UNDERSTANDING
THE KABBALAH

BY EDWARD ALBERTSON

Complete I Ching

Prophecy

Seances and Sensitives

Spiritual Yoga

Understanding the Kabbalah

Understanding Zen

Vedanta

EDWARD ALBERTSON

Understanding

The Kabbalah

For The Millions Series
Sherbourne Press, Inc. — Los Angeles

FIRST PRINTING

Library of Congress Catalog Card Number 00-00000
ISBN 0-8202-011406

Composition: Omega Repro, Tarzana, CA

PRINTED FOR
SHERBOURNE PRESS
BY
R. R. DONNELLEY & SONS COMPANY
THE LAKESIDE PRESS

CONTENTS

TO ARTEMIS

not the Goddess of Ephesus, nor of the Moon,
nor of the hunt, but of this house.

FOREWORD

IN ANY STUDY of comparative religions, it is essential
to distinguish between the occult and the mystic, both
of which may lead to the Goal Supreme, but by very
different paths. The line between occult and mystical
philosophies is not only slender, it is irregular and
blurred, and although it is possible to define the two
with a pair of rather broad definitions, these do not tell
us all we need to know.

The occult may be seen as a field of spiritual en-
deavor that focuses upon gathering and storing masses
of factual data, leading to an increased, if not total,
comprehension of truth. The mystical concentrates
upon certain spiritual exercises and disciplines, the mas-
tering of which leads to knowledge of the truth.

All well and good. But problems arise when these two
fields begin to approach each other, and even to overlap,
as when the mystic practices a particular ritual, or the
occultist sits in meditation. And the problems are com-
pounded when we come to see that most, if not all,
major religions have both occult and mystical aspects. In
Hinduism, there is the Tantra, the occult path, and
Yoga, the mystic path. In Buddhism, we have the extremes of the Tibetan Tantrists and the followers of
Zen.

The great religion of the West, Judeo-Christianity—
the combination of the Old and New Testaments into

one Bible is no accident—also has its occult and mystical facets. There are a number of passages in the Old Testament that, properly understood, are pure occultism. We first come upon one of these in the Fourteenth Chapter of Genesis, repeated in greater detail in the New Testament in Hebrews. The story concerns the defeat of a coalition of kings by Abraham, after which he is rewarded with a blessing by Melchisedec, King of Salem [Sholem?], "which is, King of Peace." (7:2) We read further, in Hebrews 7:3, that Melchisedec was "Without father, without mother, without descent, having neither beginning of days, nor end of life; but made like unto the Son of God; abideth a priest continually." Just prior to these verses, in 6:20, we read, ". . . Jesus, made a high priest for ever after the order of Melchisedec." We also find in the earlier account in Genesis, that "Melchisedec king of Salem brought forth bread and wine," for Abraham, the first appearance of what was to become known as "The Lord's Supper."

Consider these facts: that Jesus was said, by Paul, to be of "the order of Melchisedec," not of Aaron, the first high priest of the Exodus, as one might have expected; that the Last Supper, or Eucharist, is a magic rite, belonging to the classification of the occult, for what else is the transubstantiation of bread into flesh and wine into blood, but magic? And isn't Melchisedec, birthless, deathless, without parents or offspring, an occult figure?

Mystics seek the direct knowledge of God, or Truth, by a direct path; the true mystic cares little for gods, or sons of gods, for rites or miracles. These are the meat and drink of the occultist. The popular image of an occultist is that of a sage surrounded by heaps of dusty tomes, studying the mysteries of alchemy, magic geometrical figures, the Tarot, astrology, and the like. The mystic, on the other hand, is pictured as sitting calmly in meditation and completely at rest. A less dramatic image, it is true, but who is to say which of these, the occultist or the mystic, is closer to his goal?

The Kabbalah, a term covering every school of Jewish mysticism and occultism, is, therefore, similar to all other religions in which the goal is an immediate and personal knowledge of Reality. It might seem strange to the average reader to speak of Jewish mysticism and occultism, since the popular concept of Judaism is one of a legalistic sort of faith, girt about by the *Mishna* (text) and *Gemara* (commentary) of the Talmud, the digest and interpretation of the Torah, the Old Testament of the Christians. And it is true that the Talmudists set about an almost nit-picking task of ferreting out obscure meanings of words, and even individual letters, in order to insure that God's Holy Law would not be violated through ignorance. But while this was going on, there were those who, while holding all due reverence for the Law, felt that there was more to religion than mere searching for legalistic dicta.

The earliest known group of Jewish mystics were the *Hasidim* (pious ones), who preceded Christianity, and, in fact, from whom the Essenes and Pharisees were offshoots. Philo of Alexandria said in *Quod Omnis Probus Liber* that they were "eminently worshippers of God, not in the sense that they sacrifice living animals (like the priests in the Temple), but that they are anxious to keep their minds in a priestly state of holiness."

And there were other early mystics, one notable group being that based on the first chapter of Ezekiel, which tells of his vision of the heavenly chariot *(Merkabah)*. We will examine some of these sects, or branches, or orthodox Judaism in the chapters that follow.

CHAPTER 1

THE HIDDEN KNOWLEDGE

EVER SINCE THE middle ages when Jewish occultists impressed and frightened Europe with their powers of summoning spirits (demons) and their prowess in alchemy, the Kabbalah has been a watchword of mystery. Those outside the circle of Judaic religion knew of its existence, had heard countless speculations about the secret knowledge it was said to possess, but knew nothing concrete about the Kabbalah. They did not even know that it was many texts, written down at different points in history, nor were they aware that the various authors were for the most part merely transcribing an oral text of still later antiquity. What the Kabbalah is, where it can be found, and the kind of knowledge that it possesses have remained generally unknown. In fact, today and in former times, the greater number of Jews are almost as ignorant of the contents and practices of the Kabbalah as their Gentile contemporaries.

Where there is mystery, there are rumors. And rumors about the Kabbalah ripple through the conversations of students of mysticism and the occult. It is said by occultists and mystics that none but a Jew can grasp hold of the intricacies of Kabbalistic texts. Others say no, the Kabbalah is there for the Gentile, too, but first he must learn Hebrew and then he must be prepared to devote his life to the study. And it is said that even when these conditions are met, they may result in disaster for many a student of the Kabbalah has met with an untimely and unpleasant death on a spiritual equivalent of a bad LSD "trip."

Like most rumors, these contain partial truths, the bits of factual information creating more confusion than if the rumors had been wholly composed of falsehoods. The most misleading of the partial truths whispered about the Kabbalah is its identification with the occult.

The first and foremost goal of the authors of the Kabbalah was to remove the barriers between man and the Godhead. Most of the students of the Kabbalah are those who seek knowledge of God and those who love God without knowing.

However, it is true that certain knowledge about and psychic nearness to the Godhead produces (rather as a side effect) powers that are often called occult. And it is true that portions of the Kabbalah, which are often referred to as the "practical" Kabbalah (*Kabbalah Maasit*), that largely deal with occult practices.

The remainder is called the contemplative Kabbalah (*Kabbalah Iyynit*). But the differentiation is a matter of degree. All the texts of the Kabbalah contain knowledge about the Godhead, means of reaching toward the Godhead, speculations about the Godhead's relationship to creation, and man's relationship to the universe and to the Godhead.

Teachers of the Kabbalah confirm the rumor that those who enter the study of the Kabbalah for the sole purpose of gaining "practical" knowledge and "practical" powers often come unaccountably to grief. However, the same teachers also point out that students with the highest ideals and only scorn for "practical" purposes come to grief.

For this reason in the beginnings of its history, the knowledge of the Kabbalah was literally hidden, passed from the lips of a teacher to the ear of a disciple, its existence never suspected by the majority of law-abiding Temple-goers or even by many of their rabbis. The discipline of secrecy was strict. The Haggidah imposed the rule: "It is forbidden to expound the first chapters of Genesis to two men (at the same time), and it may be expounded only to one by himself. It is forbidden to expound the Merkabah even to one by himself unless he be wise and filled with understanding." In the Babylonian Torah the reason for this rule is illustrated by a story: "A certain young man expounded the Hashmal when he was consumed by fire. When one asks the question, Why did this happen? The answer is given: He was not prepared."

Mystics of religions through the world have given similar warnings and prohibitions. There are objects, incantations, and ceremonies too sacred, that is to say too powerful, for the unprepared person to handle or say or participate in without harm to his body or his psyche or both. Such an injury is no more a punishment than the fall we experience when we disregard the laws of gravity or the radiation burns we would suffer if we approached an unshielded atomic pile.

The charge that Kabbalists kept their knowledge hidden in order to maintain their corner on the market in occult knowledge is false and unfair. They imposed the cumbersome discipline of secrecy on themselves to protect the ignorant from harm. Every master of the Kabbalah knows of those who gained an intellectual perception of its teaching without the necessary foundation of character change or those who pursued a path not intended for them who met with disaster. Their secrecy was and is a safeguard like a fence around a swimming pool or a lock on a guncase.

This point is difficult to understand for those of us raised in an age and place in which God is not much thought about or believed in; or when He is, He is felt to be something of a cross between a pal and Santa Claus.

The men who put together the knowledge of the Kabbalah knew something about the Godhead. Not very much, perhaps, in relationship to the totality. But they knew enough to realize that the final reality of God was beyond man's understanding. And they knew enough to know that the power that radiates from the Godhead is beyond man's enduring unless it is received at a great psychic distance or "veiled" by psychic obstacles.

Most—though not all—mystics throughout historic time agree on this point. Even among the number who began by worshipping an anthropomorphic diety, many ended by recognizing that the deity they loved was a veiled glimpse of the greater reality.

Many have been so fascinated and dominated by the wonder of the greater reality which they had discovered by meditation or which had been found as though by revelation that they willingly chose to abandon their personality and ego, abandon life as we know it, to merge into the Godhead. This was the goal of the Buddhists and of Vedantists. But the Kabbalists had a different goal.

The Kabbalists were struck with awe and wonder speculations and distant visions of the Godhead. They believed it was the goal of every human soul to be united eventually with the Godhead. They believed, as do the Vedantists and the Buddhists, that the union could occur only when the soul had perfected itself in life or in many lives here on earth. The Kabbalists chose to devote themselves to helping all mankind reach that perfection. They used their own spiritual strengths to teach and to strengthen others. And while they taught and served as an example, they tried to discover as much about the Godhead as it is possible for a human to know and to creep as close to the Godhead as possible.

That was their goal. In the beginnings nothing was written down. (The literal meaning of the word Kabbalah is "that which is received.") The disciple received the teachings from the master. Then in turn his pupil received it from him. In those early days, there was no single term for the Kabbalists. They were called The Understanding Ones, The Masters of Knowledge, The Children of Faith, Those Who Know Wisdom.

However, the series of crises which beset the Jews beginning with the fall of the second Temple threatened to cut the heritage of hidden knowledge by killing off the teachers before they could finish training their disciples. To prevent this loss, some of the masters began putting down their knowledge in manuscript form, ignoring the advice and overriding the protests of many of their peers.

The likelihood is that many teachers after much meditating on the problem decided that the cure was more dangerous than the threat and refused to take the risk. As a result of such decisions much knowledge may have been lost to mankind; and the haunting possibility remains that some hidden lines of mystic discipline escaped the persecutions and pogroms that have plagued the Jews through the centuries and still are being secretly learned and handed down from teacher to pupil.

By the fourteenth century, the term Kabbalist was the customary designation for these teachers of the hidden knowledge and the Kabbalah was the collective term used to refer to the existing manuscripts of that knowledge.

Once knowledge has been put into manuscript form it has a life of its own. No longer has the teacher the same ability to select who shall receive it or how it shall be used. A thousand accidents can take the manuscript out of the teacher's hands and put it into the hands of an over-eager student, an irreverent materialist, a shallow man greedy for power, a stranger possessing more curiosity than is good for him, or an illiterate who destroys it or carelessly passes it on.

In the passage of time all of these possibilities were realized, not once but over and over. In the end, the body of written knowledge known as the Kabbalah became public property.

Fortunately there is a second way in which the Kabbalah's knowledge is hidden. It is secret knowledge because even when its text is held and read, the deepest and truest meanings are not apparent. In that way it may be likened to the Godhead that is its subject: there are many layers of meaning within it. All are true, but some are higher and greater truths and hence more hidden than others. In order to protect the innocent, the authors of the written texts hid the most powerful truths beneath symbol and myth and anagram and complex formuli.

The Kabbalists left a map to their treasure, but part of the map is written in code and the code must be broken before it can be understood. While the rumor that claims only a Jew can understand the inner meanings of the Kabbalah is false, it is true that much of the code only can be broken by those well versed in Hebrew. For that reason the body of this book concerns itself with an understanding of the parts of the Kabbalah where language is no barrier.

The way of the Kabbalah requires strength of purpose and body, keenness of wit; it requires the soul of a mystic but a bookkeeper's capacity for discipline.

Today, hereditary schools exist, dating from the fourteenth century and perhaps even before, dedicated to help a select number of students help break the code of the texts of the Kabbalah. Usually these schools require that a man be married, that he have obtained a certain age, and that he be judged by his teachers to be psychologically sound and of good character.

The requirements of the schools are so stringent, the demands on the students' time and energy so great, that one wonders at the enrollment. Beginning such an aescetic study would be absurd were it not for one shining enticement: properly used, the Kabbalah has proved to be remarkably effective.

Effective for what? In its purest use, the use of its original intent, the Kabbalah is a group of instructions to help the individual push aside the veils in order to see the Godhead more clearly, to remove the obstacles between himself and the Godhead, to enlist him in the effort to help all human souls perfect themselves that mankind and the Godhead at last are reunited.

Because omnipotence and omniscience are part of the glory of God, occult knowledge and power radiate upon the successful journeyman. Used as they were meant to be used, this knowledge and power are merely means of preparing the individual for still closer glimpses and greater appreciations of that goal. The holy men who are adept in the Kabbalah do not speak of knowledge and power, they speak of joy and they concern themselves with becoming and remaining in harmony with as much of the Godhead as it has been permitted them to understand.

There have been those who had the wit to decipher the code of the Kabbalah and gained possession of some of the knowledge and power it describes only to become possessed by it. For some, the worst that happened was that they progressed no further toward the Godhead. Many experienced more serious consequences. This is the warning that must be given to all who try to decipher its code: the Kabbalah is for only the foolhardy and the adament.

Those who are one or the other can look for the texts of the Kabbalah within the compass of Judaic sacred writings. Because these manuscripts were written in code, even learned scholars of the Kabbalah dispute among themselves over the exact composition of its table of contents.

Some hold that the Kabbalah begins with much of the Talmud and the Torah. Others restrict the Kabbalah to the Sepher Yetzirah or Book of Creation, the Zohar, and the Commentary on the Ten Sephiroth. The term "Kabbalistic writings" also includes commentaries on these books by the great teachers of the schools of the Kabbalah.

So it is that the Kabbalah is not a single text and not even a single system of knowledge but a multiplicity of different approaches to the same goal. The library of Kabbalistic literature still is growing and will continue to grow. To present in a short space a valid summary of these approaches and discussions is impossible.

Nevertheless, one can present a number of statements with which most Kabbalists would agree and go on from there to a detailed consideration of a Kabbalistic discipline from which the non-Hebrew-speaking layman can profit.

Kabbalists may be called mystical agnostics. They

perceive that the absolute reality of God is boundless in nature. He cannot be understood by the human mind even in ecstatic meditation. This absolute reality they refer to as Ein Soph (the infinite).

The Kabbalist Baruksh Kosover said "Ein Soph is not His proper name, but a word which signifies His complete concealment. . . . And it is not right to say 'Ein Soph, blessed be He' or 'may He be blessed' because He cannot be blessed by our lips."

Ein Soph as such did not create the universe. But from Ein Soph issued ten emanations or Sephiroth which are both finite and infinite. From these emanations the different worlds gradually evolved.

The first manifestion of God from Ein Sof is Ayin or Nothingness. God who is called Ein Sof in regard to Himself is called Ayin in respect to His first revelation. Azriel, another Kabbalist, taught that this first Sephirah is always within the potentiality of Ein Sof.

It was the Sephiroth who created human souls in their own image. And it is the Sephiroth who is God the Father of the Bible. Human souls are destined to return to the Infinite Source from which they emanated. To do so they must develop all those perfections the germs of which are already within them. Until the soul completes its development, upon the death of the body, it must migrate into another body. When all human souls that were created by the Sephiroth have perfected themselves, the restitution of all things will take place. Hell will vanish. Once again Satan will become an angel of light. And all souls will return to the Deity from which they emanated. And from that point on the creature shall not be distinguished from the creator.

CHAPTER 2

ORIGINS

THE TERM KABBALAH comes directly from the Hebrew word meaning "tradition," and signifying "traditional doctrine." This, by itself, should tell us something of the antiquity of the Kabbalah and the very depths of its roots in the fertile soil of Jewish religion since, with the Jews, traditions are not formulated easily. They come slowly, handed down from one generation to another after having been pondered, mulled, and considered. All this *before* anything is written down.

When the first Kabbalists emerged, how, then, were they able to give emphasis to the beginnings of this profound and intricate mystical tradition? Since there was no apparent or available tradition from which to interpret, didn't they, indeed, have to start out afresh?

The answer to that is an emphatic yes according to Dr. Gershom G. Scholem, the ranking modern scholar of Hebrew mysticism. But even the manner in which the Kabbalists began is of interest because it, too, shows a reverence for tradition. Here are the early mystics, located in time at the tail end of the twelfth century, devout and orthodox Jews who had a voice that did not reflect the very orthodox channels they sought to expound upon. But there were revelations that drove these pious ones onward, and the revelations that came to them were, in essence triggered by the very traditions to which they clung with such tenacity. The tradition was born then because of the fact that these early mystics had heard a voice and were devoting themselves to the interpretation of that voice according to the precepts and tenets that had been set forth in earlier revelation.

Clearly the most important of all revelations and traditional channels for the orthodox Jews were to be found in the Torah, which in itself was law and history, a tradition to be interpreted and lived and studied.

The Kabbalist rabbis and thinkers saw the Torah as having a three-fold reality that included the concept of the use of God's name as the highest concentration of divine power, the concept of the Torah as a viable organism that unfolded more of its mystery and power with study and preparation, and the principle of the infinite meaning of the divine word as expressed through revelation.

For years, centuries, Hebrew mystics have tried to bridge the gap between magic, the attainment of powers, and mysticism. The use of divine power from key or seed names was fanned in the Kabbalistic studies and it was believed that this power brought forth more of the vision or revelation to the beholder from the divine nothingness that we shall investigate in these pages.

The Torah was elevated by the mystics to a position of divine power, offering more than a way and ritual— offering in addition a complex fabric of information that would allow the individual to hear as it were the intonation of the divine words as uttered by God.

The infinite meaning and variation of the Torah, a mystical notion that sprang directly from the very awe-inspiring power and nature of the contents of the Torah led—and we are cutting directly and perhaps a bit sim- plistically to the point—to the creation of the *Zohar,* and other written literature. This literature dealt with the esoteric and exoteric interpretations of the Torah. "In many passages of the *Zohar,*" Dr. Scholem writes, "the principle is developed that the Torah is at once hidden and manifest ... the author [of the Zohar] finds this dualism not only in the Torah, but in every conceivable sphere of existence, beginning with God and embracing every realm and aspect of Creation."

The *Zohar*, a three-volume work that seeks to show the foundation for the cosmic architecture of the Most Mysterious Powers, is the exact opposite of the Talmud, which advises that the individual confront life on an earthly, simplistic basis. The *Zohar* begins by asking questions about The Creation. How did it begin? How did it look? How did it work? How did it grow? And before it finally concludes, says Michael Horowitz, a young countercultural writer of philosophy, "it has evoked an entire spiritual world system—a world system that works to explain the emanation of sacred energy from the infinite to the humblest person."

Supporting the concept of the hidden, esoteric meanings concealed in the Hebrew holy writings, this passage from the *Zohar*:

> Woe to the man who sees in the Torah only simple recitals and ordinary words! Because, if in truth it only contained these, we would even today be able to compose a Torah much more worthy of admiration. For if we find only simple the words, and we would only have to address ourselves to the legislators of the earth, to those in whom we most frequently meet with the most grandeur, it would be sufficient to imitate them and make a Torah after their words and example. But it is not so. Each word of the Torah contains an elevated meaning and a sublime mystery. The recitals of the Torah are the vestments of the Torah. Woe to him who takes this garment for the Torah, itself! It is with this meaning that David has said: "O YHVH, open my eyes to the end that I may contemplate the marvels of thy Torah."

As an indication of the allegorical character of the Zohar and, parenthetically, as an offering to scotch any remaining argument that this document is to be interpreted on a literal word-for-word basis, this extract:

Like unto a beautiful woman hidden in the interior of a palace, who when her friend and beloved passes by, opens for a moment, a secret window, and is seen only by him; then again retires and disappears for a long time: so the doctrine shows herself only to the elect (that is, to those devoted to her with soul and body), but also not even to these always in the same manner. In the beginning, deeply veiled, she beckons to the one passing with her hand; it simply depends if in his understanding he perceives this gentle hint. Later she approaches him somewhat nearer, and whispers to him a few words, but her countenance is still hidden in the thick veil, which his glances can hardly penetrate. Still later she converses with him, her countenance covered with a thinner veil. After he has accustomed himself to her society, she finally shows herself to him, face to face, and intrusts him with the innermost secrets of her heart. He who is thus far initiated into the mysteries of the Torah easily comprehends that all those profound secrets are already based upon the simple sense of the word and are in harmony with it from which not a single yod is to be taken or added.

The authorship of the *Zohar* is an insoluble problem for scholars, although a multitude of them have tried. It has been attributed to the Rabbi Simeon ben Yohai, who lived in the second century of the Christian Era, and purports to be the result of a divine revelation. It has also been said to be based on traditional conversations between God and Adam in Heaven. The *Zohar* is supposed to have been found in a Galilean cave in the thirteenth century, where it had been hidden, much as was the case with the Dead Sea Scrolls, which were found in the caves around Qumran.

True, the *Zohar* first appeared in Spain during the thirteenth century, but scholars agree that it could not have been written much earlier. It is also shown that it was not written at any one time by any one author, but is a conglomerate of many faiths and philosophies, chiefly the Torah and Talmud, but with foreign accretions of non-Jewish thought, principally Neo-Platonism and Gnosticism. To the mixture, Jews of Persia added a sort of Judaized Sufism.

The thrust of the *Zohar* is somewhat different from that of the more orthodox Talmudists, who concentrated upon the letter of the Law, as can be seen from this quotation attributed to Simeon ben Yohai: "Woe unto the man who sees in the Torah nought but simple narratives and commonplace words. . . . Every word in the Torah contains a higher meaning and a sublime mystery."

It is this higher meaning of the Law which is the true one. The *Zohar* insists that there is an inner as well as an outer reality in all phenomena. These different levels of reality arise because the physical universe results from a series of emanations, or precipitations, one from another, having their source in the Divine Being.

The *Zohar* also contains a mass of medieval astrology and Pythagorean numerology which may seem out of place in a scripture, the main teaching of which is propounded at a most profound level. There is also a good deal of the text having to do with reincarnation, which is an essential part of the *Zohar* and the Kabbalah.

The second of the texts important to the Kabbalah is the *Bahir,* or "Brilliant," in all probability the product of Nahmanides (1194-1270), a famous scholar, or by his teacher, Ezra. However, Heinrich Graetz, the noted German Jewish historian of the nineteenth century, says that the author of the *Bahir* was Isaac ben Abraham of Posquieres, usually known as Isaac the Blind, a French Rabbi of the twelfth and thirteenth centuries.

The most important of the Kabbalistic works is the *Sepher Yetzirah,* or "Book of Creation," its date is also uncertain, but it has been fixed at some time before the beginning of the second millennium. It has been attributed to Abraham, who would seem to be a rather unlikely source, and to the even more unlikely Adam, who must have been employed in more mundane activities after the Lord told him: "In the sweat of thy face shalt thou eat bread." It is more probable that the author was Rabbi Akiba, who lived in the first century of the Christian Era. Again, however, this date must be viewed with some suspicion as being too early.

The *Sepher Yetzirah* introduced the concept of the *Sephiroth*, the ten potentialities that were latent in the Infinite until emanated by Him. In the *Zohar*, this concept was further developed, as in the following passage: "The Ancient One, the most Hidden of the hidden, is a high beacon, and we know Him only by His lights, which illuminate our eyes so abundantly. His Holy Name is no other thing than these lights [the Sephiroth]."

These texts propounded the theme of the three levels of non-manifestation. The first of these may be a bit difficult to comprehend. It is called the Ayin which has been translated as "Negativity," in the sense that nothing affirmative can be stated about the Supreme Being. However, the term might be objected to on the grounds that it implies an absence of existence, a non-being rather than a non-manifestation. I believe that a more suitable word is the one employed in Zen, "The Void." In one of his verses, Nagarjuna (c. A.D. 150) explains that this is not a total emptiness, but an emptying of all concepts about Reality and Truth from the mind, which cannot grasp them anyway. He says:

> One cannot say it is void or not-void,
> Nor is it both, nor neither.
> But so that we may refer to it,
> We call it "The Void."

The *Ayn,* then, is that level so far beyond our powers of conception that we cannot even begin to think of its true nature, if it can be said to possess a nature.

It has also been called "The Absolute," but this word would imply that we have some understanding of it and are expressing that understanding in positive terms, whereas, whatever it is, it cannot be expressed at all. To express is to define, and to define is to limit; and we who are finite, cannot encompass, nor express, the Infinite.

The second of these levels is the *Ein Soph,* which literally means "No End." Thus, the *Ein Soph* may be called "The Infinite," or "The Boundless." But, having given it a name, we still do not understand it. It is so far beyond our poor powers of comprehension, that we can only speak of it in negative terms; we cannot say what it is, but only what it is not. The following passage is taken from the *Zohar:* "Before He had created any shape in the universe, before He had created any form, He was alone, formless, resembling nothing. Who could perceive Him as he was, before creation, since He was without form? . . . Such is the meaning of the words [Deuteronomy 4:15] : 'For ye saw no manner of similitude on the day that the Lord spake unto you in Horeb out of the midst of the fire.' "

The third of these levels is the *Ein Soph Aur,* "The Light Without End," or "The Infinite Light." Being infinite, it has no circumference and, therefore, no center, but out of itself is created a center, *Kether,* which will be the subject of further discussion when we come to the Tree of Life, of which it is the topmost part. This is the light that the aspirant sees when he has reached the highest state of mystical consciousness, the *Samadhi* of the Hindus, *Satori* of the Zen Buddhists, and the illumination of the Western mystics. The phrase "to see the light" has been corrupted to mean "to understand," but it stems from this illumination in which one understands the Reality of the universe.

The *Ein Soph Aur* is in many ways similar to "The Word" in the Gospel according to John, as well as to the Hindu *Om.* In Aramaic, this word is "Memra," the term bequeathed by Jonathan, son of Uziel, the greatest of the disciples of Hillel the Elder (30 B.C.–A.D. 10). It is an attempt—and a very successful attempt, as this author sees it—to explain how the Void, which can certainly feel no need to take action, such as creating a universe, does indeed take such action through one level of its total being.

This mysterious Infinite, this inexpressible All, this unspeakable Beingness, which we have called "The

Void," may be approached by two paths, the mystical and the occult. And here we must beg to differ with the dictum of Immanuel Kant: It may be unknown, but It is certainly not unknowable. The mystic may know It through any one of a number of methods or disciplines, principally those of the four Yogas: *Bhakti Yoga*, the way of love and devotion to God; *Karma Yoga*, the way of selfless work; *Jnana Yoga*, the way of discrimination between the Real, God, and the unreal, all else; the *Raja Yoga*, the way that combines the best of the others. There is also Zen, and both Judeo-Christianity and Islam have their mystical practitioners.

The occult ways are also many and varied, but the one with which we are about to deal offers the best and simplest method for the Westerner to follow. It is more direct and contains a far smaller amount of incomprehensible verbiage than do some of the other systems, notably Theosophy. And, unlike those systems, it provides a map of the terrain over which we must pass. When correctly used, a map is the most valuable adjunct of the traveller's kit, and all those who would traverse the Kabbalah have such a map.

> Oh, Traveller of the Hidden Way,
> Beset by snags and snares most rife,
> Pursue thy course, let come what may,
> Well-charted by the Tree of Life.

CHAPTER 3

OTZ CHIIM

THE *OTZ CHIIM,* Hebrew for the Tree of Life, is no tree at all, but rather a pictograph. It is a representation of the spiritual nature of both the universe and man by the use of a combination of symbols.

It consists of ten circles, or centers, such a center having the Hebrew name of Sephirah. The ten Sephiroth (plural of Sephirah) are arranged in such a manner that they can be connected by twenty-two lines, known as Paths. And that is about all that one sees when he first looks at the *Otz Chiim.* At first glance, there does not seem to be very much to detain us; a group of circles connected by some lines. Surely, there can't be anything of interest here.

Let us, therefore, look at another symbol, this one in the field of physics: $E=MC^2$. Nothing very prepossessing about that, is there? Just three letters and a digit, with an "equals" sign thrown in. Of course, we now know that upon this little symbol, the whole enormous world of nuclear physics was founded. It may have little meaning for the layman, but in the hands of a scientist, it is the basis for a level of energy far beyond anything previously dreamed. We are now living in the Atomic Age, whether for good or ill, all because of that simple little $E=MC^2$.

So, perhaps we should not merely glance over the Tree of Life, and then pass on, as if it had no message for us. We might be missing out on a good thing.

THE TREE OF LIFE

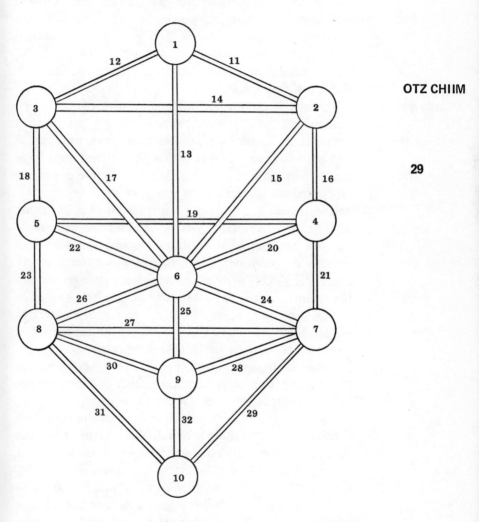

Figure 1

Those learned Rabbis who have spent the better part of their lives contemplating the Kabbalah and the *Otz Chiim,* have said that the Sephiroth are the Ten Holy Emanations, meaning that each Sephirah emanates from the one above it, the topmost being the First Emanation of the Ein Soph Aur, Kether. We are told that Kether is still above the comprehension of the normal human mind, to be realized only in the highest state of enlightenment, when it becomes the doorway to the Void, itself. It has been called the Arcane of the Arcane, the Hidden of the Hidden.

Perhaps it would be more descriptive of the actual process to use the word "precipitation," rather than "emanation." The example has been given of a pan of boiling water, to which sugar has been added until there is a supersaturated solution. When no more sugar can be caused to dissolve in the water, it is allowed to cool, and as it does so, the sugar is forced out of the solution and begins to crystallize. It is a fascinating experience for one first seeing this almost magical appearance of crystals out of water that seemed to be as clear as any other water. Out of the formless, form emerges; out of the unmanifested, manifestation is created. This is as opposite an illustration of the emergence of Kether out of Gin Soph Aur as can be given by physical means. If one were to actually perform this experiment, he would gain an even better concept of the process, totally beyond the level of conception, which occurs when the Infinite Light crystallizes out the Kether.

And this process is repeated as each of the Sephiroth precipitates the ensuing Sephirah. God, according to the Kabbalah, does not create the universe level by level, moving from one step, so to speak, down to the next. Creation takes place with the first crystallization into Kether, and the rest follows out of necessity. We might choose another simile, that of a chain of basins connected by a channel. As the first basin is filled with water, becoming a pool, it finally overflows and the excess water runs down into the next pool, which overflows in turn, filling the next, and so on.

Creation, then, is not the handiwork of a personal God who fabricates every blade of grass, every flower, every tree, and every human, but rather the result of the Impersonal precipitating out if Its own Being that which becomes the created universe. This is where the Kabbalah differs from religion taught in the regular churches and synagogues, and even in most of the temples of other faiths. The usual teaching is that of some Divine Spirit who, on a certain day, decided to make the stars, planets and other heavenly bodies, and to fill His favored planet, the Earth, with a variety of vegetable and animal life. Particularly in the Judeo-Christian religion, of whatever sect, the chief among these animal forms, man, is a born sinner, having inherited this unhappy trait from his remotest ancestor. While the Hindus, Buddhists, Mohammedans, and Taoists are not so eager to declare themselves sinful, most of them do think of creation as the result of the efforts of one or more gods.

The Kabbalists say that there may be gods, but these are also creatures rather than creators, having been the result of creation just like the rest of us. The idea of a personal God building His universe piece by piece, has been the cause of an enormous delay in the advancement of science, and those early scientists who tried to overcome this barrier in their search for knowledge were considered as heretics and severely punished for their pains. It was not until the nineteenth century breakthrough of such concepts as evolution, and the consequent overthrow of ecclesiastical rule over men's minds, that the great scientific progress of modern times could take place. And yet, the ancient Kabbalah had been teaching the concept of evolution for many centuries.

Mention has been made of the twenty-two paths connecting the Sephiroth; these correspond to the twenty-two letters of the Hebrew alphabet, each of which has an occult meaning and a numerical value, they also correspond to the twenty-two trumps of the Tarot pack. It now becomes plain that there is much to be considered, pondered, and finally realized about each of these paths.

The path, itself, between any two Sephiroth must be contemplated in the light of those Sephiroth, each Sephirah having its own significance, and the combination of the two generating an entirely new significance. Added to this, one must then take into account the numerical value and occult meaning of the Hebrew letter and the Tarot trump. All of this must be thoroughly digested and the essence of it distilled before the particular path may be understood and its message made clear.

While we have been speaking of twenty-two paths, there are actually thirty-two; ten additional ones are the Sephiroth themselves. Although a center can hardly be considered a path in the same sense that the paths are connections between the centers, each Sephirah contains within itself a path. Unlike the connecting paths, these generate their own significances without modification.

As if these were not a sufficient number of complications, we must also take into account the four worlds, or perhaps it would be better to say the fourfold nature of the world. These are: *Atziluth,* the Divine World, the Prototypal World, or World of Emanations; *Briah,* the World of Creation, the World of Pure Nature, sometimes called *Khorsia,* the World of Thrones; *Yetzirah,* the World of Angels, the World of Formation; and *Assiah,* the World of Matter, the World of Action. Each of the Sephiroth exists on all four levels and manifests through each of them. In Atziluth, they manifest through the ten Holy Names of God. (These names will be given when we come to the discussion of the individual Sephiroth.) In Briah, the manifestation is through the Ten Mighty Archangels, whose names will also be given later. In Yetzirah, the manifestation is through various orders of Angels, the Hosts of Angels. In Assiah, the manifestation is through what are called the "Planetary Spheres."

Before discussing the individual Sephiroth, we shall first look into the Three Columns along which they lie. These are found on the Tree of Life, but must be diagrammed differently in order to avoid confusion.

THE COLUMNS

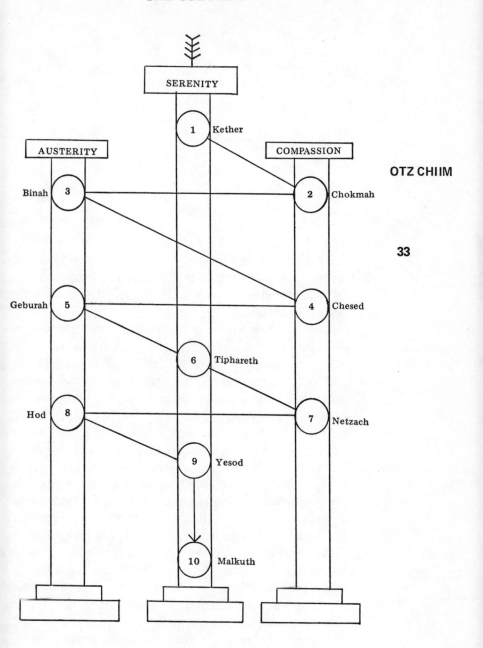

Figure 2

CHAPTER 4

THE COLUMNS

THE TEN SEPHIROTH are arranged in three columns; the central column has the attribute of Serenity, and is known by that name or as Mildness. The column on the left has the characteristic of Austerity. The one on the right is Compassion.

The columns are considered this way when we are observing them as a representation of the universe. However, "as above, so below," we may also apply the pictograph to ourselves, and when we do so, we no longer are looking *out* at the universe, but *in* toward our own natures. Then we must reverse the order of the columns, as though we were backing into the Tree of Life, at which point, left becomes right, and *vice versa*.

At the head of the central column, Serenity, is Kether, already mentioned as the first precipitation of Ein Soph Aur. Kether, in turn, to use the illustration of a series of pools, overflows into the second Sephirah, Chokmah. As the translation of Kether is the Crown, so Chokmah means Wisdom. The overflow now proceeds to the third Sephirah, Binah, or Understanding.

Kether, Chokmah and Binah, form a triangle, called the Celestial, or Supernal, Triangle. There is a fourth Sephirah, one not shown in the pictograph, since it is considered to be in a different dimension. It is called Daath, which means Knowledge. It occupies the region between Chokmah and Binah, but may be said to be the apex of a pyramid of which the triangular base consists of the Celestial Triangle. It can be said that the original precipitation, wisdom and understanding combine to produce knowledge. This, of course, is not factual knowledge, but the supreme knowledge of realization. Remember, Daath is not shown on the pictograph, nor is it counted as one of the ten Sephiroth.

The fourth Sephirah depicted is Chesed, or Mercy and Love. It is found in the right column, that of Compassion, below the second Sephirah, Chokmah.

The fifth Sephirah is Geburah, or Strength. It is in the left column, that of Austerity, below the Sephirah of Binah. There is no Sephirah in the center column on the same plane with Chesed and Geburah.

The sixth Sephirah is Tiphareth, Beauty; it is found in the center column, below the level of the fourth and fifth Sephiroth.

The seventh Sephirah is Netzach, or Victory. It is in the column of Compassion, on the right, below Chokmah and Chesed.

The eighth Sephirah is Hod, or Glory. Again, the center column is not represented at this level, and Hod is found on the left, Austerity, below the Sephiroth of Binah and Geburah.

The ninth Sephirah is Yesod, or the Foundation, found on the center column of Serenity.

The tenth, and final, Sephirah is Malkuth, the Kingdom. It is also on.the center column, below Yesod.

These are the Sephiroth of the *Otz Chiim,* ten of which are visible, and one invisible.

Although we are not yet ready to discuss in detail the individual Sephiroth, we can look into their characteristics as suggested by their locations on the columns.

On the Column of Serenity, in the center, we find the Sephiroth Kether, the Crown; Tiphareth, Beauty; Yesod, the Foundation; and Malkuth, the Kingdom, in the order of their descent.

The Sephiroth of the center column also symbolize the levels of consciousness. The lowest, Malkuth, depicts sense perception, an awareness limited to the material world. Yesod is the core of the astral being, the seat of the psychic life. Tiphareth is the higher mental, or spiritual level, sometimes called "The First Initiation," the point from which the spiritual aspirant begins his life as a true Yogi. Kether, as we have noted, is the highest illumination.

The path of the mystic is straight up the column of Serenity; it is steep and difficult. There are no resting-places for the weak and weary, the faint-hearted will be discouraged. Almost all will fall back at times, some clear to the bottom. But all who persevere will accomplish the climb eventually.

The path of the occultist rises from Sephirah to Sephirah. Like the winding road up the face of a mountain, it is less steep than the direct ascent, but it is also less hazardous. Those who fall back, do not fall as far, perhaps only until they land upon the next lower Sephirah. Those who choose this way also gain certain occult powers, and when they reach the higher realms, may become great magicians. The followers of the mystic path gain few occult powers, with the possible exception of some psychic talents when they attain Yesod, or the astral level.

We have seen that each of the Sephiroth exists in the four worlds: Atziluth, Briah, Khorsia and Yetzirah. They may also be grouped individually in these worlds. Thus, Altziluth, the Divine, or Prototypal, World, contains but one Sephirah, Kether. Briah, the World of Creation, contains Chokmah, Widsom, the Celestial Abba, or Father, and Binah, Understanding, the Celestial Ama, or Mother. Yetzirah, the World of Formation, consists of Chesed, Love; Geburah, Strength; Tiphareth, Beauty; Netzach, Victory; Hod, Glory; and Yesod, the Foundation. Assiah, the World of Matter and Action, consists solely of Malkuth, the Kingdom. Malkuth is actually four Kingdoms, those of Air, Fire, Water and Earth, the Elements of creation, the building blocks of the material universe which have come down through ever more material levels, until they appear, at least to us, as totally physical.

There is an additional grouping which must be taken into consideration, under the headings of what are called the "Three Mother Letters" of the Hebrew alphabet: *Aleph*, A; *Mem*, M; and *Shin*, Sh. These letters symbolize the elements Air, Water and Fire respectively. In the Airy Kingdom of Aleph we find the triad of Kether, containing the root of Air, descending through Tiphareth into Yesod. In the Watery Kingdom of Men is its root, Binah, descending into Chesed and Hod. In the Fiery Kingdom of Shin is Chokmah, the root of Fire, descending through Geburah into Netzach. Tiphareth is the Solar Fire and Yesod the Lunar light; Binah is the Great Sea, *Marah*.

So the Sephiroth may be grouped according to their placement on one of the three columns, or in one of the four worlds (although we must not lose sight of the fact that each Sephirah exists in all four worlds), or in one of the three Kingdoms, *Aleph, Mem* and *Shin*.

We are now to see that there is an additional grouping, one that is perhaps more significant than any of these. Let us not become impatient with what may seem to some as a series of unnecessary complications, for it must be remembered that while each Sephirah has its own importance, our understanding of it is vastly increased by a knowledge of its associations with the others. It is as though a Sephirah contains an involved significance, much of which is concealed from us until evolved by our comprehension of its interactions with each of the remaining Sephiroth.

If the proverbial man from Mars were to come upon a rubber tire, he might study it, inside and out, until he obtained a great deal of knowledge about it, but he would still know only a small fraction of what is to be known about tires until he could see it mounted on the rim of an automobile wheel, which in turn would be affixed to that complex piece of machinery, consisting of motor, gears and the rest, and also see the car in operation. Then, and only then, would he understand the nature and purpose of that rubber object he had discovered.

CHAPTER 5

THE TRIANGLES

IN SPEAKING OF the columns, we took note of the first three Sephiroth, Kether, Chokmah and Binah, and mentioned that they formed a triangle, called the Celestial, or Supernal, Triangle.

The Celestial Triangle, consisting of the Crown, Wisdom and Understanding, and the mysterious and invisible Death, Knowledge, pertains quite clearly to the head, and in fact, the Kabbalists, including the Rabbis who developed and expounded the philosophy, have referred to it by such other titles as the White Head and *Arik Anpin,* the Vast Countenance. MacGregor Mathers says, "The symbolism of the Vast Countenance is that of a profile in which one side only of the countenance is seen; or as it is said in the Kabbalah, 'In him is all right side.' " The left side is ever invisible, turned as it is toward what the Buddhists call "the Void."

Kether, the Crown, is not actually a part of the head, but reposes upon it. It does not enter into manifestation except as it generates Chokmah and Binah. It is the capstone of the pyramid of which Chokmah and Binah are the two manifested base angles and Daath the third, unmanifested, base angle.

In the Rabbinical literature, Chokmah is called *Abba,* the Celestial Father, and Binah *Ama,* the Celestial Mother. Thus, from the Crown descends the male principle, the creative initiating force, strong and active, and

THE THREE TRIANGLES

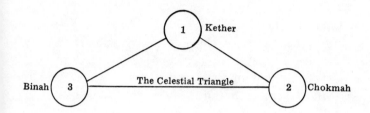

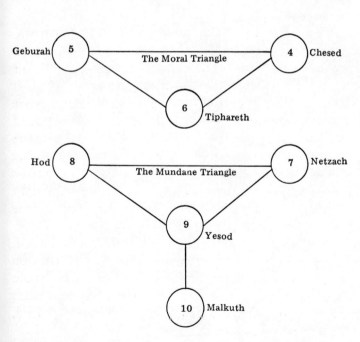

Figure 3

the female principle, the receptive sustaining force, yielding and passive. These two forces, when seen in their true perspective, are not in opposition, but are like two sides of the same coin. As it is said in the *I Ching:* "The Creative and the Receptive must combine in order to generate the visible universe." [See this author's *The Complete I Ching,* Sherbourne Press, 1969.]

There are also astrological aspects of the Triangles. Kether is called Primal Vortex, the First Swirlings, and Chokmah the Zodiacal Sphere. Binah is *Shabathai,* Saturn, and each of the descending Sephiroth, as we shall see, has its own planetary sphere. Saturn is the Latin equivalent of the Greek Kronos (time), and the father of Jupiter, Neptune and Pluto, as well as several other gods. As the father of the gods, it is fitting that Kronos, or Saturn, should be the first of them to be placed in the Otz Chiim, and that his planet should also be the first.

We must pause at this point to examine an ancient and very true philosophical concept: there can be no physical universe until the Absolute has somehow become differentiated into the Father and Mother principles. Consider the Hindu idea of *Maya,* a word stemming from the root *Ma,* to measure. Maya is also the Mother of the Universe, out of which has been created all that exists on a physical level. Kapila, the founder of Sankhya, one of the six systems of Hindu philosophy, says, "When the gunas [inertia, activity, and passivity] are in a state of serenity and equilibrium, there is Maya without name or form. When the gunas cease to be in that state, the universe is brought forth."

If we apply this statement to the Otz Chiim, we see that equilibrium is the state of the central column of Serenity, and the universe is brought forth as we descend into the lower Sephiroth of Chokmah and Binah, swinging first from one column, that of Compassion, to the other, that of Austerity. Thus, the universe is created by the disequilibrium caused by the projection, or descent, of Kether into Chokmah and Binah, and the other Sephiroth are the precipitations of these.

In the context of the Father-Mother principle, it is interesting to note that all the Avatars—those incarnations of God in the form of man, such as the Christian Jesus, or the Hindu Krishna—have their female companions. There are Jesus and His Mother, Mary; Rama and his wife, Sita; Krishna and his playmate, the *gopi*, or milkmaid, Radha, and many others, all illustrating the idea that the male principle, in and of itself, is powerless to create without the receptivity of the female. When Brahman, the Impersonal Absolute, is separated from Maya, his *Shakti*, or power, the world comes into being. Perhaps it is confusing to say "separated," and we should substitute the phrase "considered separately." Brahman and his Shakti are One, and cannot be separated any more than fire and its heat, water and its wetness, or copper and its conductivity.

The Second Triangle might be called the Moral Triangle, or the Triangle of Virtue. It consists of the Sephirah Chesed, precipitated by Binah, and it in turn precipitates Geburah and Tiphareth. Chesed, Mercy, is below Chokmah on the column of Compassion; Geburah, Strength, Severity, is below Binah on the Column of Austerity, and Tiphareth, Beauty, is the next Sephirah under Kether, on the column of Serenity, or Equilibrium.

Chesed is also called Gedulah, Majesty or Greatness. It is the planetary sphere of Tzedek, Jupiter, the equivalent of the Greek Zeus, son of Kronos, whom he overthrew. He thus became the Lord of Heaven.

Geburah, also known as Pachad, fear. Its planetary sphere is Madim, Mars, the Greek Ares, son of Zeus and god of war.

Tiphareth, the sixth Sephirah, has the planetary sphere of Shemesh, the Sun. The Sun, as we know, has been considered as a god in many religions, being Ra of Egypt, Surya in India, Helios in Greece, Ormuzd in Persia and Tezcatlipoca in Mexico.

The Second Triangle, it will be seen, faces in the opposite direction from the First, having its point down. There is, thus, a most important distinction noted between the two. In the First Triangle, the two opposites, Father and Mother, Creativity and Receptivity, are generated from the first Sephirah; equilibrium is differentiated into activity and passivity, or as the Hindus would put it, Sattva is manifested by its projection into Rajas and Tamas.

The Second Triangle displays just the reverse: the pairs of opposites, Creativity and Receptivity, return to rest in Equilibrium; Father and Mother project their Son. For this reason, the Kabbalists sometimes refer to Tiphareth as the Redeemer, the Savior. When the Redeemer is sacrificed, as all the avatars have been, then equilibrium is restored.

Between the First and Second Triangles lies the Abyss, not to be crossed by the human living a usual mundane life. When meditating upon the Otz Chiim, as will be discussed in a later chapter, one may raise his consciousness up the central path to Tiphareth, through love and devotion for God, and there he will enjoy a deeply moving spiritual experience. But in order to raise himself into the First Triangle, and thence to Kether and the infinite illumination of the *Ein Soph Aur,* one must traverse the Abyss, and he will find no easy bridge by which to cross over. It has to be taken at a single bound, ignoring the fancied peril of a fall into that Abyss, and this may only be done after he has become an habitual resident in the Sephirah Tiphareth.

Behind and below Tiphareth, running clear across the Tree of Life, is Paroketh, the Veil of the Temple, It separates the Second, Moral, Triangle from the Third, as the Abyss comes between the First and the Second. Below the Veil lie the centers of every day consciousness. Here we find the vast majority of mankind, those who attend to their earthly affairs, alternating between the pairs of opposites, good and evil, love and hate, vice and virtue, occasionally giving a thought to the things of the spirit, but seldom giving them more than a passing thought.

One who wants to rise above the mundane world must first rend the Veil of the Temple. As we read in

Mark, 15:38: "And the veil of the temple was rent in twain from the top to the bottom." The veil was a curtain in the temple at Jerusalem that separated the oracle, containing the Ark of the Covenant, from the sanctuary. Only the priests could enter the sanctuary, and only the high priest the oracle. The symbolism is apparent: only the pure aspirant may enter through (rend) the Veil of the Temple.

Most mystical religions have one or more avatars, or Redeemers, and one who rends the Veil of the Temple, thus entering into the sphere of Tiphareth, will see him. So we read, in John, 14:8,9: "Philip saith unto him, Lord, show us the Father, and it sufficeth us. Jesus saith unto him, Have I been so long time with you, and yet hast thou not known me, Philip? he that hath seen me hath seen the Father; and how sayest thou then, Show us the Father?" The message is clear: he that enters into Tiphareth, has a vision of his Redeemer, and his vision is also one of the Father, Chokmah.

The Biblical account of the rending of the Veil is most likely in reference to the rending of Paroketh, rather than the physical veil in the temple of Jerusalem. The human mind has a veil that separates the worldly from the spiritual, permitting the worldly man to rest comfortably in his mundane pursuits. One does not fall into the spiritual state by accident, but must make an effort to attain it. And it is this effort which may be called "rending the Veil of the Temple." Tear away the barrier of Parakoth, a barrier that proves quite flimsy when attacked, and one may enter onto that path of which the first habitation is Tiphareth.

And so to a consideration of the Third Triangle, which may be called the Astral-Physical Triangle, since the dweller in this Triangle spends his waking hours on the physical plane, and his sleeping hours on the astral, and never rises above them. It might also be called the Mundane Triangle. It is composed of the Sephiroth Netzach, Victory; Hod, Glory; and Yesod, the Foundation.

Netzach, Victory, and sometimes Firmness, has the

planetary sphere Venus, the Greek Aphrodite, daughter Jupiter (Zeus) and Dione.

Hod, Glory, has the planetary sphere Kokab, Mercury, the Greek Hermes, son of Jupiter.

Yesod, the Foundation, has the planetary sphere of Levanah, the Moon, ruled by Diana, the Greek Artemis.

It would seem at first glance that we have here reversed the usual masculine-feminine relationship established by the first two Triangles; Father and Mother in the Celestial Triangle, and repeated in the Moral Triangle. But such is not the case. Each Sephirah is both masculine and feminine, positive and negative, standing as feminine in regard to the Sephirah from which it is generated, the one just preceding it, and as masculine to the one it in turn generates, that which follows it.

Therefore, each Sephirah is, to borrow a phrase from astrology, well-aspected when it functions in harmony with the column in which it is located. Thus Chesed, Mercy, is well-aspected in the role of the just father, tempering justice with mercy, but ill-aspected as the sentimentalist, seeking to preserve those things which should better be disposed of by its opposite on the right-hand column, Geburah, Strength. The sentimentalist, the so-called "humanitarian," is, perhaps, the greatest sinner against the Universal Plan, which includes, as the Hindus tell us, the Trinity of Brahma, the Creator, Vishnu, the Preserver, and Siva, the Destroyer. The universe must not only be created, but preserved, and when it has outlived its purpose, destroyed in order to make room for a new universe.

It is important, however, to understand this doctrine fully; not all destruction is beneficial, far from it, and not all preservation is the result of sentimentality. When a fresh universe, a fresh nation, a fresh social order or a fresh idea that is constructive has been created, it must be preserved for as long as it remains constructive. Only when it ceases to be of benefit to mankind, should it be allowed to decay and fall into.destruction. By the middle of the Third Century, the Roman Empire had become overripe for its fall, and when Alaric finally took and sacked Rome in 410, it was not so much his prowess as a soldier, but the Empire's decadence that led to its destruction. This decadence is easily explained, being a combination of sentimentalism and greed, the sentimentalism of the "humanitarians" and the greed of the politicians for public support. For the first six hundred years of its history, Rome was composed of hardworking and hard-fighting citizens, men who contributed something of value to their republic. But as the farmers began to leave their land in the wake of several long and costly wars, and move into the City, they found great difficulty in securing employment. Rather than return to their farms, they formed a mob, the proletarians, and the "humanitarians" began to open the Empire's treasury to them. Slowly at first, but in ever greater volume as the politicians discovered that the mob's votes could be purchased for a loaf of bread, the "welfare class" began to grow. In making every effort to enlist the proletarian votes, entertainment was added to the food handouts, until "Bread and Circuses" became the first concern of the elected officials and later, the Emperors. Another word for Bread and Circuses is "socialism," which can lead only to the total destruction of any society. This is the inevitable round of all civilizations: creation, expansion, decay, destruction; the one following the other as a planet follows its star.

And lastly, we come to Malkuth, the Kingdom, which has no planetary sphere, but is the sphere of the Earth elements: Earth, Air, Fire and Water. Lest there be some misunderstanding, it might be well to state here that these elements are not those of physical science, which consist of ninety-two elements found in nature, but the states or conditions in which all the elements exist. Thus Earth refers to all those elements that exist in a solid state, the minerals as a rule. Air covers those elements that are gaseous in nature, and Water, those that are liquid. It was also noted, in the ages preceding written history, that the above elements, or at least many of them, contained the ability to burn when ignited. Fire was supposed to be an element of these substances; a thing could not burn unless it already contained the element of fire.

This concept was refined by some unknown ancient into one holding that the four elements were not the physical ones from which they took their names, but the spirit or essence of those things. Thus Water was not used to refer to liquid substances, but to the subtle quality of liquidity or wetness.

Physical science recognizes the elements of the Kabbalists as solid, liquid, and gaseous, with electricity and atomic fission and fusion corresponding to Fire. These, then, are the states of the Earth sphere, Malkuth, the tenth Sephirah. It is the lowest on the Tree, and is not part of any Triangle, although it is the recipient of the influence shed upon it by the other nine. If we will return to our imagery of the series of basins, one overflowing into the next, we will see that what finally reaches Malkuth has passed through all the others. From Malkuth, one may make his spiritual journey either up or down, upward toward Kether, or downward into the realm of the demonic Sephiroth, properly called the Qliphoth. We will deal with these in a later chapter.

CHAPTER 6

THE TREE AND
THE WORLD

IN THE FIFTEENTH chapter of the *Bhagavad Gita,* the most beloved scripture of the Hindus, we may read of the Vedantist version of the Otz Chiim, the Tree of Life:

> The rishis tell us of the tree,
> Asvattha, heaven-rooted, trunk
> Below. Each leaf sets forth
> The Vedas. Who knows this, knows all.
>
> Its branches spread from high to low,
> By Gunas fed. The senses, buds,
> Which, blooming in the world of men,
> Create desires and worldly lives.
>
> Asvattha is by men unseen,
> They know it not, source, root nor branch.
> Who takes the non-attachment sword
> And hews it to the very root.
>
> Attains the goal that he has sought
> And, thus, is never more reborn.
> Take refuge in that Primal One
> From which there flows the stream of life.

The followers of the Vedas are more of a mystical disposition than are their brothers, the followers of the Kabbalah, as the above verses show. Mystics tend to pursue a course leading to the dissolution of the physical universe, insofar as its hold on them is concerned, while the occultists feel that the path leads through the material world and must be traversed step by step. Strangely enough, although the mystic and the occultist tread seemingly incompatible paths, both are right; both paths will lead them to the goal. Sri Ramakrishna once said, "Let each man follow his own path. If he is sincere in his desire to know God, he will surely realize Him."

The verses from the *Bhagavad Gita* were quoted not in order to create some controversy, but merely to show that the Tree of Life is to be found in many otherwise divergent religions. In the Biblical story of Adam and Eve, we read, "And the Lord God said, Behold, the man is become as one of us, to know good and evil: and now, lest he put forth his hand, and take also of the tree of life, and eat, and live for ever: Therefore the Lord God sent him forth from the garden of Eden, to till the ground from which he was taken. So he drove out the man; and he placed at the east of the garden of Eden Cherubims, and a flaming sword which turned every way, to keep the way of the tree of life."

This story of the fall of man is filled with occult symbolism, and much is to be learned from a careful consideration of it. The Lord did not at first forbid Adam to eat of the tree of life, but only of the tree of the knowledge of good and evil. Presumably, it would have done no harm if Adam had eaten of the former, until he had eaten of the latter. In other words, in his original state of innocence (which also means "ignorance") he could have been immortal. But once he had "become as one of us"; that is, become like a god, immortality was not safe for him.

In an ancient manuscript in the Library of the Arsenal at Paris, there is recounted the experience of Seth, Adam's third son, who made his way to the gate of the garden of Eden, where the angel with the flaming sword permitted him to see the tree of life and the tree of knowledge grafted upon each other, an occult way of saying that science and religion were made one in the

Kabbalah. This manuscript, *The Book of the Penitence of Adam,* proceeds to tell how the angel gave Seth three seeds from the Tree, which he was to place in Adam's mouth after his death. Seth did as directed, Adam was buried, and there resulted a bush, the burning bush from which God spoke to Moses. From this bush, Moses took a small branch, out of which he fashioned his wand. This was later placed within the Ark of the Covenant, and was finally planted by King David on Mount Zion, where it grew into a three-stemmed tree. King Solomon cut it down to form the two pillars which were placed at the entrance to the temple and the third trunk was fashioned into the threshold. This is where the aspirant stands when he becomes a candidate for admission to the mysteries, the two pillars and the candidate becoming the three columns of the Otz Chiim. This threshold was removed by certain temple priests opposed to the Kabbalah, weighted with stones and sunk in the temple reservoir. However, the reservoir was drained in the time of Christ, and the beam was discovered and taken to be made into a bridge across the brook Kedron, over which Jesus crossed on His way to Gethsemane. The bridge was then taken up by the Roman soldiers to make the cross upon which Christ was crucified.

This allegory illustrates the idea that the tree which caused the fall of Adam furnished the cross from which he ascended into Heaven. Or, to put it in the terms of an old saying: "Man fell in Adam and was raised in Christ." Properly viewed, the fall of Adam is not a cause for lamentation. Mankind must pass through three states: innocence (ignorance), knowledge and resurrection. While knowledge, particularly of a mundane nature, may seem to be a fall from the state of innocence, it is a necessary step on the path to liberation. The innocent have no need of salvation, and would not know that there even is such a thing. The child does not know that saints exist and has no desire to become one.

The best example of an innocent is a child, playing its childish games, its mind without blot or blemish. But the child is also ignorant, which is not a fault, and is not something for which to blame him. It is his natural state. Before he can aspire to illumination and liberation, he must first become a man, with a man's responsibility for his actions. Only when he is able to see what is right and what is wrong, can he take measures to correct his faults and to reach out toward his own salvation.

The so-called "fall of man" is written for all to see in the pictograph of the Otz Chiim. That which is to become a man descends from Kether, through Sephirah after Sephirah, until it reaches Tiphareth. Remember that Tiphareth, having been precipitated by the preceding Sephirah Geburah, is in its negative aspect, not in its role as the Redeemer, but as the innocent Adam, not yet descended or "fallen" into mortality. At last, yielding to that power which drives us all toward the ultimate goal, man reaches out for knowledge and falls out of Eden. Dwelling in the lowest Triangle for a time, perhaps that of many lives, he at last feels the urging to peer beyond the Veil of the Temple, and once moved in this direction, rends the Veil and comes back to Tiphareth, the first step on his road to the supreme knowledge. Having examined the Tree of Life in its relation to our world, we now turn to a more profound study of the Tree as it is applied to the Four Worlds.

As Erich Neumann points out in *The Great Mother*, a Bollingen Series work devoted to the investigation of primordial archetypes, "The tree plays an important role in the Kabbalah as tree of life and sephiroth." Many important cultures provide tree symbols as manifestations of a system with roots in the earth, branches aspiring to—and reaching—heaven. Neumann's point about the tree symbolism is illustrated with a quote from the Book of Bahir, an early Kabbalistic text:

> It is I who planted this tree that all the world might delight in it, and made it an arch over all things and named it "universe," for on it hangs the universe and from it the universe emanates; all the things have need of it and behold it and tremble for it; it is thence that the souls emanate.

Interestingly enough, it is not only the fact that the tree has branches reaching heavenward that interest ancient and modern Kabbalists, or, indeed such "friends of the court" as Carl Gustav Jung; it is precisely because the tree has roots sinking deep into the earth. So far as Jung, to a lesser extent Freud, and others preoccupied with myth, the depths, the darkness and earth in which the roots are sunk signify the unconscious.

Many Kabbalists, past and present, while not using precisely these terms, are curious about the implications about that area we now think of as the unconscious, they think of it as a potential seat of power, of mystical insight, and as a rich area from which to draw more of the complex meaning and symbolism to be found as the Kabbalah's mysteries unfold before them.

Now, let's look at the worlds in which the Sephiroth are found, and how the tree symbol applies.

CHAPTER 7

THE TREE AND
THE FOUR WORLDS

WE HAVE PREVIOUSLY had a brief discussion of the Four Worlds: *Atziluth*, the Divine World; *Briah*, the World of Creation; *Yetzirah*, the World of Formation, and *Assiah*, the World of Matter and Action. The Ten Sephiroth exist on each of these, although on a different level. What we have heard concerning the Sephiroth up to this point, has applied chiefly to the Divine World, Atziluth, which is also called the World of Emanations. Now we are to look at the three other Worlds or spheres, and we may be a bit confused at first to see that the Sephiroth appear on each of these in the same pictograph, but on a lower level of manifestation.

We have treated Malkuth as the lowest Sephirah, the last to receive the precipitation that began with the overflowing of Kether. Now we are to see that this Malkuth precipitates the Kether of Briah, followed in order by the other Sephiroth until the Malkuth of Briah precipitates the Kether of Yetzirah, and the Malkuth of Yetzirah precipitates the Kether of Assiah. The Malkuth of Assiah is just above the Qliphoth, the beginning of the demonic world.

Atziluth, the Divine World, differs from the others in still another way: it is the only one of the Worlds upon which God acts directly, while the others are acted upon by His emissaries. Those who carry out the Divine Will in Briah are the Archangels, in Yetzirah the Angelic

Hosts, and in Assiah the Zodiak, planets and Earth elements.

Each of the Ten Sephiroth in Atziluth has its own form of the Divine Name, which should not surprise anyone who has read the Bible, since it gives many names for the Supreme Being: God, Lord, the Lord God, Heavenly Father, etc. One might think that these were used merely as an author's artifice to escape endless reiteration of one Name, but such is not the case. The Names are very precise occult terms by which the particular facet of the Infinite to which one is referring can be made known.

It is to be remembered that each letter of the Hebrew alphabet has a numerical equivalent and so the Divine Names are also rather complex occult mathematical equations forming a system known as Gematria, upon which was founded ceremonial magic and the Tarot. We have previously seen that there are twenty-two paths joining the Sephiroth, a number equaling the letters in the Hebrew alphabet, so that each of the Divine Names is also a formula composed of several paths.

The Divine Names of the Sephiroth in Atziluth are these:

Kether——Eheieh
Chokmah——Jahveh
Binah——Elohim
Chesed——El
Geburah——Elohim Gebor
Tiphareth——Tetragrammaton Aloah Va Daath
Netzach——Jahveh Tzabaoth
Hod——Elohim Tzabaoth
Yesod——Shaddai el Chai
Malkuth——Adonai Malekh or Adonai ha Aretz

In the above, Eheieh has a very profound meaning. It is the word heard by Moses "out of the midst of the (burning) bush." We find it in Exodus 3:13,14: "And Moses said unto God, Behold, when I come unto the children of Israel, and shall say unto them, The God of your fathers hath sent me unto you; and they shall say to me, What is his name? what shall I say unto them? And God said unto Moses, I AM THAT I AM (Eheieh)."

Jahveh, or more properly JHVH, is God the Father, who said, "Let there be light." Elohim, the word appearing in the first verse of Genesis, is translated as "God," but in Hebrew, it is a feminine noun with a masculine plural suffix, and should, therefore, be read in that context as: "In the beginning the Gods and Goddesses created the heaven and the earth."

Tetragrammaton Aloah Va Daath may be translated as "God made manifest within the mental sphere." Jahveh Tzabaoth means "The Lord of Hosts" and Elohim Tzabaoth means "The God of Hosts." Shaddai el Chai is "The Almighty Living God." The two Divine Names of Malkuth, Adonai Malekh and Adonai ha Aretz, mean "The Lord Who Is King and the Lord of Earth."

As was noted above, only in the world of Atziluth does God act directly. In the world of Briah the Archangels preside as emissaries of the Most High. These are:

Kether——Metatron
Chokmah——Ratziel
Binah——Tzaphkiel
Chesed——Tzadkiel
Geburah——Khamael
Tiphareth——Raphael
Netzach——Haniel
Hod——Michael
Yesod——Gabriel
Malkuth——Sandalphon

In some of the texts, there are slight differences in the Archangelic names: Metratton for Metatron, Sabbathi for Tzaphkiel, Gamaliel for Khamael, and Jesodoth for Sandalphon. Also, in at least one of the texts, the positions of Haniel and Michael are reversed.

These are the members of the Angelic Hosts who preside over the World of Yetzirah:

Kether——Chaioth ha Qadesh
Chokmah——Auphanim
Binah——Aralim
Chesed——Chasmalim
Geburah——Seraphim
Tiphareth——Malachim
Netzach——Elohim
Hod——Beni Elohim
Yesod——Kerubim, or Cherubim
Malkuth——Ashim

The meanings of these terms are: Chaioth ha Qadesh, Holy living creatures; Auphanim, wheels; Aralim, thrones; Chasmalim, brilliant ones; Seraphim, fiery serpents; Malachim, messengers; Elohim, gods; Beni Elohim, Sons of God; Kerubim, the strong ones; and Ashim, Souls of Fire.

In the World of Assiah, as has already been noted, the emissaries are the Zodiac, planets and Earth elements, all of which were given with the listing of the Sephiroth in the chapter on the Triangles.

Mention was made earlier in this chapter of the word we utter as "Jahveh," but which is actually spelled JHVH, or in Hebrew, Yod, He, Vau, He, since Hebrew has no vowels in its alphabet. No one, not even a Rabbi, can pronounce JHVH correctly unless the correct articulation of the word has been transmitted to him by someone who has had it passed down to him. This is the reason that the Sacred Name of God cannot be uttered, except by the holiest of men, and they never speak it aloud unless it is to communicate it to a deserving and righteous pupil. JHVH is the true Tetragrammaton, the Word of Four Letters, and it is the most arcane of the Mysteries.

All quaternary (fourfold) groupings are classified under the headings of the four letters of the Tetragrammaton, and it is important to the occultist to discover these so that their interrelationships may be understood. Such a grouping is that of the Four Worlds we have been examining. Another is that of the four elements, and the four triplicities of the signs of the Zodiak, and the four suits of the Tarot pack. These divisions lie respectively in the fields of the Qabalists, the Alchemists, the Astrologers and the Diviners.

We know very little if we are told that one of the Sephiroth is named Geburah. We learn little more if we are told to examine this Sephirah in the World of Assiah. However, we begin to gain some comprehension if we discover that its planetary sphere is Mars, of the triplicity of Fire, ruler of both Aries and Scorpio. And if we understand the Tarot, or if we will take the trouble to learn something of it, we will learn even more from our knowledge that its suit is that of Swords.

This, then, is the way to study a Sephirah; and they should be studied one at a time at first, for it is to little purpose to begin comparing them and trying to establish their relationships until we have a fair grasp of what each of them has to tell us. Constantly and gradually we build our knowledge if we wish to be occultists, for occultism is the way of knowledge.

CHAPTER 8

THE INDIVIDUAL SEPHIROTH

THE TEN SEPHIROTH are intermediaries between the unknowable and invisible Deity and the material which may become knowable and visible to mankind. The Zohar, itself, is a source of discussion for the relationship of the Ten Sephiroth to the Ein Soph.

More recent Kabbalists advise us to consider that the Sephiroth are always thought of as a unity, a second divine unity, that of number, and also as being inherent in the Supreme Absolute Ein Soph, in which number as a concept does not exist. The Ten Sephiroth are considered in this one totality as forming the Adam Illa-ah, the Heavenly Adam or Adam Qadmon, the World of Perfect ideas.

This concept is given a full and intriguing exposition by that most famous of all "Kabbalists," (in addition to his other accomplishments) C. G. Jung. Writing in *Mysterium Coniunctionis,* Jung speaks of Adam Qadmon as "the mediator between the supreme authority, Ein Soph, and the Sephiroth."

Now, let's enter into a more amplified study of the individual Sephiroth. This is by no means to be considered as a final and definitive catalogue of all that is known, since such knowledge is not static, but ever growing. It is, rather, a possibly helpful compendium of much that has become known and much that will be needed by the occult aspirant in his upward climb. The name of each Sephirah will be followed by the transliteration of its Hebrew spelling in parentheses.

KETHER (Kaph, Tau, Resh)

Kether, the Crown, (it crowns the Ego or I) resides at the top of the central column of Serenity. "It is," the Zohar tells us, "the Principle of all the Principles, the Mysterious Wisdom, the Crown of all that which there is of the Most High, the Diadem of Diadems." It represents the Infinite distinguished from the finite, and its name in the Scripture signifies, "I am," *(Eh'yeh)* because it is the existence in Itself, the existence considered in the point of view that analysis cannot penetrate it, and to which not any qualification is permitted and which absolutely does not admit of any.

Writing as far back as 1888, Isaac Myer, an American lawyer and student of the Kabbalah, said as he translated the philosophical writings of Solomon Ben Yehudah Ibn Gebriol, "In Kether is the germ and content, in harmony, of the Sacred form, the other Sephiroth surround it as if a rich shining garment. In its narrowest sense, *Kether El'yon* Crown of the Highest, is this garment. . . . It is the representative of the coalescing of the Highest with His creation and its preservation . . . to the uttermost limits of entire nature and All. A clear knowledge of Kether cannot be obtained by man in this world. It is to him even as if Ayn (nothing)."

Rabbi Gebriol, in his Kabbalistic writings, had been attempting to clarify. Attorney Myer, clearly working with ecumenical intent, saw the understanding of this aspect of the Zohar—the aspect of the Holy or Divine Nothingness—as being a wellspring of understanding for all religious philosophy, and it is one of his points that it is important to know the nature of what we, as mere mortals, cannot hope to fully fathom.

Kether is thus beyond human comprehension, not yielding to any description in positive terms. It is a state of actionless existence; the essence of being, and the reservoir from which all being flows. It stands behind manifestation without becoming itself manifest. All form stems from it, yet it has no form. All actions have their source in it, yet it does not act. All motion rises in it, yet it does not move.

The text in the *Sepher Yetzirah*, or "The Divine Emanations," says of Kether: "The First Path [Kether] is called the Venerable Intelligence or the Arcane Intelligence because it is the Light which gives the power of comprehension of the First Principle, which is beginningless. It is the Primal Splendor, since no created living being can penetrate to its essence." Kether has always been experienced by the enlightened as Light; thus the terms that are applied to the resulting state: enlightenment, illumination, etc. In the final statement telling us that "no created living being can penetrate to its essence," we find another Yogic truth: that no man can attain to the highest state and long remain in his body. This is probably the meaning of the passage in Genesis 5:22-24: "And Enoch walked with God after he begat Methuselah three hundred years, and begat sons and daughters: and all the days of Enoch were three hundred sixty and five years: And Enoch walked with God: and he was not; for God took him." This is the picture of a most devout man; he had "walked with God" during most of his life, and then "he was not." This would indicate that he had gone out of existence as an individual, since the text does not say that he was taken up into Heaven, or simply that he had died, but that "he was not." Enoch had apparently penetrated to the essence of Kether, had seen that Light, and in a flash, had come to know the Truth. He could not live after that, and in fact, had no concern about living on this Earth.

The Kabbalists have given a number of titles to Kether, among which are: the Being of Being, Arcane of the Arcane, Ancient of Days, Ancient of Ancients, the Most High, the Center within the Circle, and the Internal Light. These titles will be helpful when one comes to meditating upon the Tree.

In the World of Atziluth, Kether is invoked by the Divine Name assigned to it, Eheieh, the Absolute, All in All, eternal, changeless, as the Yogis say, "The One without a second." Before any work is done in occult magic, it is mandatory that he first invoke the Divine Name of Kether in Atziluth. We have all heard stories of magicians who have paid, and paid dearly, for their successes in achieving their desires through the use of magical formulas. The reason for this is that whatever power they withdraw from the Tree of Life at any of its points must be replaced. In attaining to their goals they have had to surrender something of value equal to that which they have received. But Kether in the World of Atziluth is different; its powers are drawn from behind the Veils of the Void, and any power a magician receives does not have to be repaid, since it is a new power drawn through the Veils into existence, and adds to the total of forces in the universe.

Meditation upon Kether in the World of Atziluth yields another, and even more valuable, result, as we fix our minds upon this high point, we begin to realize that, as the Hindus say, "Brahman alone is real; all else is unreal." We sense the unreality of the mundane world, the world of the three lower chakras. Even though we may not have the realization of Kether in this life, our consciousnesses are raised immeasurably.

In the World of Briah, power is manifested through the ministry of the Archangel Metatron, named by the early Kabbalists as the spiritual teacher of Moses. He is also called the Prince of Countenances. The *Sepher Yetzirah* says that "Malkuth causes an influence to flow down from the Prince of Countenances, the Archangel of Kether, and is the source of illumination of all the light in the universe." In other words, the lowest Sephirah on the Tree can cause the highest to shed some of its influence. The lesson is clear; not only does the Highest emanate the lowest, but the lowest can activate the Highest. On the microcosmic level, the clear indication is that while God is the creator of man, it is also true that man can appeal to God for attention.

In the World of Yetzirah, power is manifested

through the Angelic Host called the Chaioth ha qadesh, or Holy Living Creatures. In Ezekiel 1:5 we read: "Also out of the midst thereof came the likeness of four living creatures." And at verse 1.5 of the same chapter: "Now as I beheld the living creatures, behold one wheel . . ." and 1.6: "The appearance of the wheels and their work was like unto the color of beryl." The wheels are the Auphanim, the angels ruling the second Sephirah Chokmah, and the color of beryl is blue, the color assigned to Chokmah in Atziluth.

In the World of Assiah, the force is manifested through the planetary spheres, and in the case of Kether, it is the Rachith ha Gilgalim, or the Primal Vortex. Sir James Jeans, the great astronomer, postulated a universe in which at first only the sub-atomic particles, electrons, protons, mesons, etc., existed. Then, "as though stirred by the finger of God," these began to move, as in a vortex, and thus gradually to come together, forming the great galaxies, each of which may be said to be a primal vortex. That the early rabbis were able to deduce or intuit the theories which many centuries later have become accepted by science is a fact to be considered with awe and wonder.

The Aces of the Tarot cards are assigned to Kether; in Atziluth, the Ace of Wands, the root of the forces of Fire; in Briah, the Ace of Cups, the root of the forces of Water; in Yetzirah, the Ace of Swords, the root of the forces of Air; and in Assiah, the Ace of Pentacles, the root of the forces of Earth. Kether is thus seen to be the source of the elements.

The colors assigned to Kether are a brilliant white for the upper three Worlds, and a white with golden flecks for Assiah. Actually, this is not a color, but the experience of those entering into the consciousness of Kether is that of seeing a brilliant white light, the light of illumination, the Nirvana from which no man returns.

Each of the Sephiroth has a spiritual experience with which it is associated. That of Kether is Union with God.

CHOKMAH (Cheth, Kaph, Mem, He)

Chokmah, Wisdom, resides at the head of the column of Compassion. It is precipitated by Kether, and is the first member of the first of the pairs of opposites. Out of Chokmah arises Binah, and this is a possible explanation of the story of how Eve was created out of a rib taken from Adam. Chokmah is Abba, the Celestial Father, as Binah is Ama, the Celestial Mother, and the Mother takes her being from the Father.

As has been previously said, Kether stands at the source of all power coming into the universe, and this power is forever flowing into, and overflowing, the First Sephirah. The first recipient of this overflow is Chokmah. But Chokmah is not a reservoir, zealously storing up the energies that flow into it; rather it is only a way-station, so to speak, receiving and transmitting these energies on to the third Sephirah.

Kether may be considered a static, rather than a dynamic, source of energy. Having arrived at a sort of unmanifested manifestation, by the crystallization of the essence of the Ain Soph Aur, it does not take action, but supplies the motive power for action to Chokmah. In contrast to Kether, Chokmah is kinetic, that is it takes action, creating out of itself its opposite, Binah, with the energy emanating out of the Ein Soph Aur through Kether.

"In the beginning," says the First Chapter of Genesis, "God created the heavens and earth. And the earth was without form and void (the "Void"); and darkness was upon the face of the deep. And the Spirit of God (Ain Soph Aur) moved upon the face of the waters (Marah, the Great Sea, a title of Binah). And God said, Let there be light (Chokmah): and there was light. And God saw the light, that it was good: and God divided the light (Chokmah) from the darkness (Binah)." The story of creation, as it appears in Genesis, is filled with Kabbalistic allusions, some of which we shall note under the headings of the various sephiroth.

Chokmah, the Celestial Father, is the creative force,

which does not mean that Chokmah creates, but generates creation, or perhaps, fertilizes the ovum of the mother, but does not produce the offspring, so does Chokmah fertilize Binah, the receptive Mother. Without the pairs of opposites, which are opposite in their natures and functions, but cooperate in the labor of production, there could be no creation.

Chokmah is the mobilizer of creative forces, while Binah is the organizer. We might give the example of the father of a household bringing home his weekly paycheck, which represents a certain kind of creative potential, and handing it over to the mother. If she is wise, she will spend the money—exert the force—in the most creative way. It takes the combined efforts of both, the father to inject the creative energy, and the mother to direct its expenditure wisely, to make a well-run and happy home.

It may seem strange at first glance to find the Father, the Male Principle, located on the column of Compassion, and the Mother, the Female Principle, on the column of Austerity. One would certainly think that the female is more compassionate than the male. But the male precipitates the motivating idea, not yet organized into any sort of form, while the female organizes this into form, and the task of formation is one of limiting. When the sculptor begins to form an amorphous lump of clay into a figure, he begins to limit it. In fact, this may be said to be the function of a sculptor, to limit that which has heretofore known no limitation. And this calls for austerity, discipline; no latitude is left for shapeless mass.

Also, the Mother limits the potential creation of the Father by bringing it into manifestation, for all that becomes manifest must, in the end, wither and die. Nothing is constructed that is not finally destroyed. No tower is raised that will not fall. No star is born that will not burn out. The Father gives life, but the Mother gives death, for through her comes form and form is finite, and the finite cannot become infinite, and the temporal cannot become eternal. Birth can only lead to death.

One could go on at great length concerning the symbolic sexuality of Chokmah, the Shiva Lingam and the various phallic-oriented crosses. All the ancient religions have been at one in recognition of the male and female principles, and the symbology that accompanies each. Out of this has, perhaps, originated the orgiastic practices of certain sects, but these have been brought about by the profound misunderstanding of the original idea, and the correct worship of the lingam has nothing to do with lust.

The text in the *Sepher Yetzirah* says of Chokmah: "The Second Path [Chokmah] is called the Illuminating Intelligence. It is the Crown of Creation, the Unitive Effulgence, emulating it. It is set in exaltation above over every head. The Kabbalists call it the Second Glory." This, and all the other texts from the *Sepher Yetzirah,* are vague and obscure. But its meaning can be dredged up by the student. "The Second Path" means the second Sephirah; each of the ten Sephiroth is considered a path in itself, the first of the paths between Sephiroth is numbered "eleven." "The Illuminating Intelligence" is that which leads at last to the highest. We have also seen in the passage from Genesis that "God said, Let there be light," and this referred to Chokmah. The phrases "It is the Crown of Creation, the Unitive Effulgence," would seem to apply rather to Kether, but the added "emulating it," shows that Chokmah is almost the same as Kether, not yet in manifestation until its force is combined with that of Binah, and not yet a member of a dualistic system. Although few have tried to interpret the statement that "The Kabbalists call it the Second Glory," it would seem clear that this refers to the glory that is second only to that of Kether, as the experience of the Ajna chakra is second only to that of Sahasrara.

This argument is enforced by the Spiritual Experience assigned to Chokmah. As the Spiritual Experience of Kether was Union with God, so that of Chokmah is the Vision of God. This is a very wonderful experience indeed, but there is a vast difference between it and the highest. The difference may be expressed in two phrases: "I, standing here, see God there," and "I and God are one; who is there to see whom?" When one attains to the true vision of God, his whole life is changed; he will never fall into worldliness again, but be a saint in the proper meaning of that word. When one attains to the highest, as has been said earlier, he Knows the Ultimate Truth, "by knowing which, all else is known."

The titles given to Chokmah by the Kabbalists include: Power of Yetzirah; Abba, the Celestial Father; Tetragrammaton, and Yod of Tetragrammaton. The power of Yetzirah is that of the World of Formation. We have already discussed Chokmah as the Celestial Father. Tetragrammaton is, as we have seen, the four-lettered Divine Name JHVH (Yod, He, Vau, He) of which the Yod of Tetragrammaton is the first letter. Some Kabbalists teach that all things are to be found under one of the four letters.

In the World of Atziluth, the Divine Name assigned to Chokmah is Jehovah, or more correctly, JHVH, the deity who may be seen in the divine vision. It was JHVH who spoke to Moses out of the burning bush, and who gave him the tablets of the Law, on Mount Sinai.

The Archangel of Chokmah in Briah is Ratziel, who is said to have produced the four elements out of Chaos, and who was the master of Adam.

The Angelic Host of Chokmah in Yetzirah is that of the Auphanim, or Wheels, whom we have already come upon in the Book of Revelations.

The planetary sphere of Chokmah in Assiah is Mazloth, the Zodiac. As the Primal Vortex of Kether formed the basis for planetary creation, so does the Zodiac provide the stage upon which the planets are to play their parts.

The Twos of the Tarot cards are assigned to Chokmah: in Atziluth, the Two of Wands, dominion, the place of the Father; in Briah, the Two of Cups, love; in Yetzirah, the Two of Swords, restored peace; and in Assiah, the Two of Pentacles, harmonious change. The

Two of Wands, this suit being the symbol of the element of Fire, is the Lord of Dominion, the Wand acting as a phallic symbol, which has the significance of the Father, accepted without resistance by the Mother. The Two of Cups, the suit of the element of Water, is the Lord of Love; again the Father as the wooer and winner of the Mother. The Two of Swords, the suit assigned to the element of Air, is the Lord of Restored Peace. Swords, usually a symbol of the forces of disruption, is here a restoration of Serenity. The Two of Pentacles, the suit of the element Earth, is the Lord of Harmonious Change. The Twos always represent harmony, as the Aces always signify the roots of things.

The colors assigned to Chokmah are: in Atziluth, blue, soft and pure; Briah, grey; Yetzirah, an iridescent pearl grey; Assiah, white, with red, yellow and blue flecks.

BINAH (Beth, Yod, Nun, He)

Binah, Understanding, resides at the head of the column of Austerity. It is precipitated by Chokmah, the Mother created out of the Father, as Eve was created out of Adam. Thus, the Biblical story of creation is fulfilled: out of Kether, Eheieh, the Lord God, is Chokmah, Adam, made, and out of Chokmah, Binah, Eve. Out of the Absolute, the Celestial Father, and out of the Father, the Celestial Mother.

Binah completes the Celestial Triangle, composed of Kether, Pure Being; Chokmah, Pure Energy; and Binah, Pure Form. Energy and form are the primal opposites required before there is manifestation, the physical universe. No manifestation can occur under a state of equilibrium, which is Kether. Creation is the result of a marriage between energy and matter, force and form. It is interesting to note that the science of physics now treats matter as the product of energy, since matter is nothing more than conglomerations of electrons and protons, which are not material at all, but negative and positive charges of electricity. The point of interest is that the Kabbalists were saying much the same thing long before there even was such a thing as the science of physics.

Reference has already been made to Binah as the giver of birth, and consequently, the giver of death, because all things that are born must die. Thus, Binah is sometimes called the Terrible Mother, and with this the Hindus would agree. In Hinduism, the Mother of the Universe is Mahamaya, the consort of Brahman, his Shakti, or power. The visual representation of Mahamaya is the Goddess Kali, she of the frightening countenance, wearing a necklace of human skulls and a belt of human bones, her two left hands bearing a dagger and a severed human head, her two right hands granting blessings and boons, dancing upon the body of her husband Siva, who awakens to copulate with her, and create the universe anew.

The text in the *Sepher Yitzirah* says of Binah: "The Third Intelligence is the Sanctifying Intelligence, the foundation of Primal Wisdom, the Creator of Faith, its roots are in Amen." As Chokmah is Wisdom, so Binah is Understanding. But Wisdom and Understanding are interdependent, since Understanding comes with Wisdom, and Wisdom is based on Understanding. Thus, the Celestial Triangle is seen to consist of intelligence of three sorts, although the three are one: Arcane, or Hidden, Intelligence; Illuminating Intelligence; and Sanctifying Intelligence. All intelligence is but a precipitation of Kether, and one must combine Understanding and Wisdom to pierce the Hidden Intelligence, which is the state of Kether.

At first glance, the Spiritual Experience assigned to Binah is the Vision of Sorrow, and yet, what could be more fitting? One does not understand the world if he lacks that understanding which comes with the Vision of Sorrow. This is not personal grief; far from it. It is the comprehension of the true nature of sorrow, which gladdens the heart. Here is enlightenment on the path to the final illumination, what the Yogis call "The Confrontation of Kali." If we turn from the Terrible Mother of the Universe in fear and revulsion, we will not penetrate to the heart of her message, of her very nature. The worshipper of Kali so fills himself with love for her that she ceases to act as the stern disciplinarian, the mother and destroyer of mankind, and becomes the loving mother, giving birth, comforting, and finally laying to rest her beloved child. Where in all of this can there be found room for grief? It is the Mother's way, and we have only to accept it. Until we have accepted it, we will be bound to the endless wheel of birth, death and rebirth. When we see that this is Mother's universe, born out of her, existing in her, and dissolving back into her, and that this is not a matter for sorrow, which is the content of the Vision of Sorrow, then will we be free of her wheel of existence, and passing through the spiritual experience of the Vision of God, attain to the Union with God, in the state of Kether.

As is written in the *Kena Upanishad:*

> Blessed is he who, in this very life,
> Realizes Brahman. Who realizes Him not,
> Sustaining his greatest loss,
> Misses the very purpose of life itself.

The titles assigned to Binah by the Kabbalists include: Ama, the dark sterile Mother; Aima, the bright fertile Mother; Khorsia, the Throne; and Marah, the Great Sea. We have previously referred to the Father and Mother as Abba and Ama, but now we see that there are both positive and negative aspects to the Mother, Aima and Ama. Aima is the aspect of Mother that gives birth to creation, while Ama gives death. The title of Marah, the Great Sea, refers also to the Mother. Roman Catholics speak of the Virgin Mary as *Stella Maris,* the Star of the Sea, and Mary, in fact, derives from the root *marah.* The word *marah* also means bitter, and this refers back to the Vision of Sorrow, upon which the Buddha based his Four Noble Truths: there is sorrow, there is a cause of sorrow, there is a cessation of sorrow, and there is a way to find the cessation of sorrow. The cessation of sorrow is congruent with the realization of Brahman, or entry into the state of Kether.

In the World of Atziluth, the Divine Name assigned to Binah is Elohim, which, as we have noted, is a feminine noun with a masculine plural suffix, and is to be translated as "Gods and Goddesses."

The Archangel of Binah in the World of Briah is Tzaphkiel.

The Angelic Host of Binah in the World of Yetzirah is Aralim, the Thrones. One of the titles of Binah is Khorsia, the Throne. In his *De Hierarchia Celesti,* the pseudo-Dionysius, a Fifth Century Christian Mystic, names the nine orders of angels, taken from several books of the Bible. These are: Seraphim, Cherubim, Thrones, Dominions, Virtues, Powers, Principalities, Archangels and Angels. While there seems to be some confusion in his last two classes as orders of what should be orders of themselves, it is interesting to note the inclusion of Thrones.

The planetary sphere of Binah in the World of Assiah is Shabbathai, Saturn, the disciplinarian and hard taskmaster, enforcing the austerity of Binah.

The Threes of the Tarot cards are assigned to Binah: in Atziluth, the Three of Wands is the Lord of Established Strength, the fiery dominion of Chokmah having been gathered up and organized in Binah; in Briah, the Three of Cups is the Lord of Abundance, perhaps Lady of Abundance would be preferable. The suit of Cups is essentially feminine, since the cup is symbolic of the yoni in esoteric significance. The Three of Cups is thus truly representative of Binah.

The Three of Swords, in Yetzirah, is the Lady of Sorrow, depicted in the Tarot card as a heart pierced with arrows. This is reminiscent of those paintings usually called "Our Lady of Dolors," showing the Virgin Mary seated or kneeling at the foot of the Cross, her breast pierced with seven swords, emblematic of her seven sorrows.

In Assiah, the Three of Pentacles, called the Lord of Mundane Actions, is singularly suitable to the concept of Binah as the Mother of Creation at work in the World of Matter and Action.

The colors assigned to Binah are: in Atziluth, crimson; in Briah, black; in Yetzirah, dark brown; and in Assiah, grey, with pink flecks.

CHESED (Cheth, Samech, Daleth)

Chesed, Mercy, is the Fourth Sephirah, residing on the column of Compassion, beneath Chokmah. It is separated from the Three Celestial Sephiroth by the Abyss. The Celestial Triangle, as we have seen, is also called *Arik Anpin,* the Vast Countenance; the Six that are to follow are called *Adam Kadmon,* the King. There is, thus, a configuration on the Tree of great and profound symbolism, yielding much knowledge to one who can comprehend it: the Father (Kether), the King (the Fourth through Ninth Sephiroth) and the King's Bride, the Queen (Malkuth). We shall see that one of the titles assigned to Malkuth is Malkah, the Queen.

Chesed is in a very large sense, the reappearance of Chokmah on a descending level. It is Chokmah in the mid-world of lesser divinity, as represented by the Triangle of Virtue. Where Chokmah is the Heavenly Father, Chesed is somewhat less of an abstract concept. Actually, Chesed is the basis of the so-called "Hindu Trinity" of Brahma, the Creator, Vishnu, the Preserver, and Siva, the Destroyer, for in Chesed is the motivating force of these functions, while in Geburah, its opposite, is their culmination.

As Chokmah and Binah must be considered together, since neither the Father nor the Mother can produce creation alone, so must Chesed and Geburah be treated as an inseparable pair. The Deities and their consorts, Chesed and Geburah, create, preserve and preside over the dissolution of the universe. As the story goes, Brahma (not to be confused with Brahman, the Impersonal) unable to produce a viable creation by his own efforts, divides himself into Manu and Shatarupa, a man and a woman, who proceed to "be fruitful, and multiply, and replenish the earth." Then Vishnu and Lakshmi assume their task of maintaining the universe in all its parts, until Siva and Kali attend its dissolution. This is an oversimplification of the Hindu belief, but it serves to show the similarities between the Vedanta and Kabbalah.

The text in the *Sepher Yetzirah* says of Chesed: "The Fourth Path [Chesed] is called the Receptive Intelligence because in it are all the Divine Powers, and from it emanate all spiritual virtue and the highest elements of Divinity. They are precipitated, one from the other, because of the Primal Crystalization of the Celestial Crown, Kether." We have seen the three previous Intelligences, Hidden, Illuminating, and Sanctifying. We are now shown the Receptive (Feminine) Intelligence. We have been speaking of Chesed as masculine, but it is to be remembered that the Sephiroth are both masculine and feminine, and we have seen that Brahma, the Creator, divides himself into male and female in order to create.

The Spiritual Experience of Chesed is the Vision of Love.

The titles assigned by the Kabbalists to Chesed bear out the idea of love, for one of these titles is Love. The second of these is Gedulah, Majesty or Greatness, which coincides with its magical image of a mighty king, crowned and seated on his throne.

This image gives us additional insight into the nature of Chesed. The Mighty King is on his throne, a picture of the peaceful monarch, and a further sign of his peaceful intentions is that he is wearing his crown. We shall see that in the opposite Sephirah, Geburah, the image is that of the king in his war chariot. Thus we have contrasting images, each suitable to the column upon which it is located, Chesed, the peaceful king on the column of Compassion, and Geburah, the warrior king, on the column of Austerity.

It should be noted at this point that the magic symbols of the first six of the Sephiroth contain, among others, appropriate geometical figures. The symbols of Kether include the Point, a figure that has location but no dimension. A point in geometry is the starting place for all figures; it may be said that any geometrical figure is generated by a point. Starting with the point, we may begin the next step in constructing a figure, the straight line, which has not only location, but one dimension as well. One of the symbols of Chokmah is the Straight Line. We might be forgiven if we were to assume that one of the symbols of the Third Sephirah would be an extension of the line into the simplest of geometrical figures, the triangle, and while the triangle is not included as such among the symbols of Binah, we do find the Yoni and the Kteis. The first is the Hindu word for the female sex organ, and the second the Egyptian word. The Greeks sometimes referred to this part as the Delta, the equivalent of the letter "D" which takes the form of a triangle. Again, the symbol is an appropriate one for the Mother of the Universe. And so we come to our present Sephirah, Chesed, among whose symbols are the tetrahedron, the simplest of the solid geometrical figures, consisting of three triangular faces and a base, and the equal-armed cross. To continue, Geburah, the Fifth Sephirah, has among its symbols the pentagon, the pentagram, or five-pointed star, and the five-petalled Tudor Rose. And, finally, the symbols of the Sixth Sephirah, Tiphareth, include the cube, which has six faces, and the truncated pyramid, that is, a pyramid with its point removed, also consisting of six surfaces, the base, the four sides, and the top surface.

The Tarot cards are, of course, the Fours. In Atziluth, the Four of Wands is the Lord of Faultless Labor, the peaceful king, untroubled by war, governs his dominions well. In Briah, the Four of Cups is the Lord of Pleasure. We have already noted that the Cup suit is symbolic of the yoni, so that one needs hardly to seek for further explanation. In Yetzirah, the Four of Swords is the Lord of Rest from Conflict, a reinforcement of the concept of the peaceful king. In Assiah, the Four of Pentacles is the Lord of Mundane Power.

In the World of Atziluth, the Divine Name given to Chesed is El, a root word meaning God, and part of such names as Eloh, Elohim, etc., as well as a common suffix of many names, Samuel, Gabriel, Ezekiel, etc.

In the World of Briah, the Archangel of Chesed is Tzadkiel, the angel of mercy and piety.

In the World of Yetzirah, the Angelic Host of Chesed is called Chasmalim, the Brilliant Ones.

The planetary sphere of Chesed in the World of Assiah is Tzedek, Jupiter, the Latin equivalent of the Greek Zeus.

The colors assigned to Chesed are: in Atziluth, deep violet; in Briah, blue; in Yetzirah, deep purple; and in Assiah, deep azure flecked with yellow.

GEBURAH (Gimel, Beth, Vau, Resh, He)

Geburah, Strength, Severity, is the Fifth Sephirah, residing on the column of Austerity, beneath Binah and opposite to Chesed. The magical image of Geburah is that of the warrior king in his chariot, and the rule of Mars further serves to reinforce this image. Those who have been raised in the Christian ethic tend to think of the use of armed force as something evil, and for this reason Geburah has been considered as the evil path on the Tree of Life. However, the Kabbalah teaches that all of the Ten Sephiroth are equally holy, so that it becomes of the first importance to understand Geburah, which requires more understanding than do the others.

Few there are who do not enjoy a state of peace; few there are who enjoy war for the sake of fighting. When we think of Chesed, we feel content and comfortable, but Geburah troubles us. Perhaps, to paraphrase Shakespeare, the fault, dear Brutus, lies not in our Sephiroth, but is in us. The peaceful king upon his throne is very reassuring, but the time comes when our need is for a warlike king, defending us against the foe, whether from a foreign land or on our city streets. The present-day need is for justice, tempered with mercy if you will, but justice, sure and swift. We must choose between law and order, or lawlessness and disorder.

Chesed earns our love, for the king is merciful and kind, but Geburah, in the end, merits our respect, and, therefore, our love, for there can be no love where there is no respect.

Geburah has been thought of as destructive, but again this is a mistaken concept. Destruction when correctly applied signifies the tearing down of something that is useful or beneficial and this is not the task of Geburah. The Fifth Sephirah is not the Devil, luring his victims from the path of righteousness. In fact, no Devil is required to lure anyone. Those who are enticed into unholy ways have enticed themselves. Tannhauser has to go in search of the Venusberg before he can fall from grace in the arms of Venus. Geburah merely represents the state in which Tannhauser finds himself, including his equally fervid search for forgiveness.

The Bible tells us that "the fear of the Lord is the beginning of wisdom." Geburah, one of whose titles is Pachad, Fear, is that aspect of the Tree that inspires fear and awe in our hearts, and we know that fear, if not overly indulged in, can be very beneficial, lending wings to the fleeing deer, or the man chased by a tiger.

The other title assigned to Geburah is Din, Justice, and we have already seen that this is one of the great deficiencies of our time. Justice, true justice, is not to be feared by any but the unjust. The criminal is made to suffer less than his victim. Those who have cried out for mercy toward the criminal are denying mercy to the victim, and all the victims yet unvictimized. Chesed, Mercy, must be balanced by Geburah, Justice, in order for society to exist and, of course, the converse of this proposition is also true.

The text in the *Sepher Yetzirah* says of Geburah: "The Fifth Path is called the Fundamental Intelligence because it is similar to Unity, allying itself to Binah, which emanates from the primal deeps of Chokmah."

Unity, as used here, refers to the Spiritual Experience of Kether, Union with God. Thus, it is seen that Geburah is akin to Kether, but on a lower level. Geburah is also said to ally itself to Binah, and this refers to what has already been said. Binah, the Universal Mother, gives form to the energies that have poured out of Chokmah, and in thus giving birth, gives also death. But it is in Geburah, "allying itself to Binah," that the death occurs. However, the force that is precipitated by Binah into Geburah must flow by way of Chesed and, therefore, the destruction is not that of beneficial and useful things, but the dissolution of the outworn and useless. The "primal deeps of Chokmah" are from whence these forces flow. The message of the text is that Geburah is similar to Kether from whom flows the energies into Chokmah, thence to Binah, and from Binah to Geburah by way of Chesed. It is the one stream of force and is, therefore, not evil in any of the Sephiroth.

The Divine Name assigned to Geburah in Atziluth is Elohim Gebor, sometimes called the left hand of God and the upholder of the sword.

The Archangel of Geburah in Briah is Khamael, said to bring fortitude in time of war or affliction.

The Angelic Host of Geburah in Yetzirah are the Seraphim, or Fiery Serpents. In Isaiah 6, is the account of his vision: ". . . I saw also the Lord sitting upon a throne, high and lifted up, and his train filled the temple. Above it stood the seraphims: each one had six wings. . . ."

The planetary sphere of Geburah in Assiah is Madim, Mars. Here there is imposed a test which all who would climb the path must take and pass. The God of War demands courage and willingness to fight in a just cause, but the ability to fight must not be permitted to turn one into a cruel tyrant, living for violence. The balancing forces of Chesed must be brought into play to save us from self-destruction. "He who lives by the sword shall die by the sword," if the sword is wielded for unjust purposes.

The Fives of the Tarot cards have been assigned to

Geburah: in Atziluth, the Five of Wands is the Lord of Strife; in Briah, the Five of Cups is the Lord of Loss through Pleasure; in Yetzirah, the Five of Swords is the Lord of Defeat; and in Assiah, the Five of Pentacles is the Lord of Mundane Troubles. All of the Five are evil cards, and the whole suit of Swords is unfortunate, so that the Five of Swords, yields the worst of ill fortune.

The colors assigned to Geburah are: in Atziluth, orange, in Briah, scarlet red; in Yetzirah, bright scarlet; and in Assiah, red with black flecks. These colors are appropriate for a Sephirah under Mars.

TIPHARETH (Tau, Pe, Aleph, Resh, Tau)

Tiphareth, Beauty, is the Sixth Sephirah, residing on the central column of Serenity, below Kether. It is the first return of the Sephiroth to a state of equilibrium, the pendulum having swung between Compassion and Austerity since the first precipitation from Kether. With Tiphareth the worlds of the Spirit and Virtue find their fruition in the Son. Starting with the Absolute, through the Heavenly Father and Mother, and onward by way of the Kingly Father and Queenly Mother, we arrive at the Redeemer. It is also the central point of the Tree of Life, being midway between Kether and Malkuth. Tiphareth is still another central point, that of the six lower Sephiroth, which we have already seen are called the Lesser Countenance, Adam Kadmon, the King.

Tiphareth is sometimes called the Place of Incarnation, which is a singularly apropos appellation. The normal human, upon raising his consciousness to the next level above those of mundane life, is said to be reborn. It is his second birth; the Adam-man has died; the Christ-man is born. Having rent the Veil of the Temple, the spiritual aspirant has taken the first, and most difficult step, toward liberation.

The avatars rise in Tiphareth, all but one having had their beginnings there. But that one was of a different sort. Unlike the other avatars, he began his round of lives as any other man, and also unlike them, he had to struggle as hard for his spiritual attainment as any. In fact, his struggle was more intense, because his was the task of attaining to the highest peak, beyond the topmost reach to which any mortal had previously envisioned.

After six years of practicing the sternest austerities, the Prince Gautama Siddhartha took his seat beneath the sacred Bo Tree, resolved to remain there until he had attained the highest. And in one night the highest was his. He sat down a Prince; he rose up the Buddha.

While the Buddha had to take that first step by his own effort, all other avatars of whom we have heard were born at that level and contained all those above it. They were, in other words, born liberated, and if they had any spiritual task, it was merely that of realizing their own true natures. And yet, the Buddha raised himself to be the equal of Christ, Krishna, Rama, and all the rest. His struggles explain the reason for his name, The Compassionate One, for it was through struggling to achieve what the others already had that he came to his profound understanding of mankind.

One of the magical images of Tiphareth is the Child. It is the lowest point reached by the incarnated God, and having come into birth in Tiphareth, the Son of God becomes a link between human and Divine. The Child is the true son of Binah, Mary-Marah, the Great Sea, but is the precipitation of that Sephirah through its lower level emanation, Geburah, the Giver of Death. The Son of God is thus born to die, as are all living beings, but his death is ordained and dedicated to a special purpose. While still in this life, he strives to bring his kingdom up out of worldliness and carry it across the Abyss that separates mankind from illumination; he labors to "redeem" humanity, to free it from bondage, to liberate it. He is truly the Redeemer, and in the end, his life is sacrificed, loosing great forces to restore the equilibrium between the elements of the Tree.

Therefore, a second magical image of Tiphareth is The Sacrificed God, and it is this image that has become the focal point of all observances in the Christian churches. It is difficult, if not impossible, to find a church of any Christian sect that does not somewhere feature a Cross, which is not only a Christian symbol, but also one of the symbols of Tiphareth.

What Christians have not considered is the third image of Tiphareth, a majestic King, which brings us straight back to Kether, the Crown. The close tie between the Son and Kether, through Chokmah and Binah, "Our Father (and Our Mother) which art in Heaven," has been ignored. Only the link between the Son and Chesed, "Our Merciful Father," is observed. Thus, Christianity has lost its mystic way, and except in a few instances, Saints Augustine, Francis, Bernard, and Meister Eckhart, and others, there is not, and has not been for some centuries, any visible mystical teaching or practice. The Church, by concentrating upon the image of Christ as the Child and the Sacrificed Redeemer, to the exclusion of the Majestic King, has performed an even greater sacrifice, that of relinquishing the true salvation and liberation of its people.

Meanwhile, the Son stands patiently in Tiphareth, ready to lead all who come to him to the illumination of Kether. The road to Kether passes through Tiphareth, which is the meaning of Jesus' words: "No man cometh unto the Father, but by me." This is written in the Fourteenth Chapter of the Gospel According to John, who must certainly have been a Kabbalist, for he has also said in the Tenth Chapter: "I am the door: by me if any man enter in, he shall be saved." In further support of the probability that John was a Kabbalist, one might recall the statement, virtually meaningless under any other interpretation, also from Chapter Fourteen: "In my Father's house are many mansions: if it were not so, I would have told you." Is not the Otz Chiim, the Tree of Life, "my Father's house?" And are not the "many mansions" the Sephiroth?

The text in the *Sepher Yetzirah* says of Tiphareth: "The Sixth Path is called the Reconciling Intelligence, because the inundation of the precipitations are multiplied within it, for it emits its influence as a stream to fill the reservoirs of the blessings by which they are united one to another." The question immediately arises, "Why is the Sixth Path called the Reconciling Intelligence?" And the answer is simple, once we look at the Tree. It is the only Sephirah to which every path leads directly. It is in immediate contact with every one of the other Sephiroth, and thus it imparts to the four lower Sephiroth some of its own essence, as well as the essence of each of the higher Sephiroth. Tiphareth is also in the center of the surrounding five Sephiroth which, with it, have collectively been called Adam Kadmon. Receiving the "inundation of the precipitations" from the more ethereal Sephiroth, it fills "the reservoirs of the blessings" of those below it, uniting and reconciling them.

Tiphareth is the only Sephirah to have assigned to it two Spiritual Experiences, the Vision of the Harmony of Things, and the Mysteries of the Sacrificed God. Although seemingly unrelated, they are consonant to a large degree and singularly appropriate to the realm of the Son. The second of these has already been discussed in the context of the magical image of the Child and requires no further elucidation here. And in view of what has been said just above in the Yetziratic text, we should have no difficulty in understanding that upon entering into the vision of the Son, one would become fully aware of the harmony of all things, material as well as spiritual. This universe is one, having emanated from the One Source. All things are one, for there is no other. God not only reigns in His world, He has become His world. If we do not come to understand this, we have not comprehended what is meant by the precipitation of the creative forces through Kether into each of the succeeding Sephiroth. That which finally flows into the most material section of the Tree of Life is the same as that which first entered the Tree from the Ain Soph Aur through Kether.

The Hindu sage says, "*Aham Brahmasmi*—I am Brahman." Does this seem a shocking piece of egocentricity to the person raised under the Christian ethic, or the Jewish ethic, for that matter? Does he really mean to say that he is God? Yes, of course he means it. What else could he be? What else is there for anyone to be? If you are something else than God, you do not exist at all, for God is all existence. There is only existence and non-existence, the latter being merely a figure of speech, since nothing can not-exist. Would you be willing to say, "I am not God?" To say this is the only real blasphemy, for you are denying both God and yourself, and it would be absurd to deny your own existence. If you exist, God exists; if God exists, you exist. How can it be otherwise? The titles assigned to Tiphareth are: *Zoar Anpin,* the Lesser Countenance; Melekh, the King; Adam; the Son; the Man. As Kether is the *Arik Anpin,* the Vast Countenance, so is Tiphareth the *Zoar Anpin,* the Lesser Countenance. The reflection of Kether is Tiphareth; the reflection of the Father is the Son. We have already discussed the King and the Son. There remains Adam, who is also the Son, but a son who fell into the world of men by his acquiring the knowledge of good and evil. Why there should be a physical world we do not know, but the forces which flow down the Tree created it. Possibly there is some higher purpose served by materiality, something that must be accomplished for which matter, and only matter, can serve as an arena. If this be true, then man had to enter that arena and participate in the game, for life is a game that all must play. And it is through Adam that this has come about. Of course, Adam is only an archetype; there was a first man, a man who had the knowledge of good and evil; let us be content to call him Adam.

The Divine Name given to Tiphareth is Tetragrammaton Aloah Va Daath, or JHVH Manifest in the Realm of Knowledge. Daath, as we will recall, is the mysterious and invisible Sephirah on the central column between Chokmah and Binah. It would, therefore, also be located between Kether and Tiphareth. The emanations from the Crown pass down through Knowledge into Beauty. All the Sephiroth on the central Column represent levels of spiritual consciousness; those on the two side Columns representing force and form, energy and matter.

The Archangel of Tiphareth in the World of Briah is Raphael. Longfellow, apparently with some insight into the true nature of Raphael, wrote, in his *Golden Legend:*

> I am the angel of the Sun,
> Whose flaming wheels began to run
>   When God Almighty's breath
> Said to the darkness and the night,
> "Let there be light," and there was light—
>   I bring the gift of faith.

We shall discover why Raphael is the angel of the Sun in a moment.

The Host of Angels of Tiphareth in the World of Yetzirah is Malachim, the Messengers. The word mala-chim is translated as "kings," and the Malachim are the kings of the forces of nature. The black magician, in trying to control these forces, may receive some tempo-rary benefit, but they are not to be really controlled, and he will soon find himself under their sway. One must, therefore, deal with the Malachim only through their ruler, Raphael, after having invoked the Divine Name of JHVH Aloah Va Daath. It is only after having meditated upon Tiphareth and made himself one with it, that the student of the Tree can deal safely with these great forces.

The planetary sphere of Tiphareth in the World of Assiah is Shemesh, the Sun. Raphael has always been called the angel of the Sun, which explains Longfellow's poem. One of the symbols of Tiphareth is the Lamen, worn on the breast of the adept to indicate the forces with which he is working. The adept performing his meditation on Tiphareth would wear the lamen of Shemesh.

Other symbols are the Cross of Calvary, the Rosy Cross, the truncated pyramid and the cube. The Calvary Cross antedates Christianity, but it has become the symbol—and a most appropriate symbol—of the Crucifixion. The Rosy Cross is an equal-armed cross enclosed in a circle and is a symbol of initiation, the circle signifying knowledge and wisdom. When the horizontal arms of this figure are broken, and pointing downward, somewhat like the two sides of the letter "A", it becomes a symbol of Satan, used in ancient rites of devil-worship. It can be seen today as the so-called·"Peace" symbol.

The truncated pyramid is a solid figure having six faces, six being the number of Tiphareth. However, the figure represents something more. In Mark 12:10 we read: "The stone which the builders rejected is become the head of the corner." And in Acts 4:11, speaking of Christ: "This is the stone which was set at nought of you builders, which is become the head of the corner." Now, the "head of the corner" cannot refer to the usual type of building, which has four corners, but a pyramid has only one head of the corner at its apex. The Great Pyramid of Gizeh lacks its head, and archeologists agree that it never had one; "the stone which the builders rejected." The other two pyramids at Gizeh have these stones.

When you add to the truncated pyramid of six surfaces the capstone of four surfaces you have the completed building. Adding to the six lower Sephiroth the four higher ones, you have the complete Tree of Life. The whole pyramid represents the perfected man, the fully illuminated soul, but in order to achieve this perfection, to Adam Kadmon must be added the Three Celestial Sephiroth.

The cube, as was said in an earlier chapter, also has six surfaces and is, therefore, the symbol of the Sixth Sephirah. But the cube is that solid geometrical figure most usually considered first when speaking of solids. Tiphareth is the gateway between the higher Sephiroth and the material world below it; thus the cube is a most suitable symbol.

The Sixes of the Tarot cards have been assigned to Tiphareth: in Atziluth, the Six of Wands is the Lord of

Victory; in Briah, the Six of Cups is the Lord of Joy; in Yetzirah, the Six of Swords is the Lord of Earned Success; and in Assiah, the Six of Pentacles is the Lord of Material Success. Even the Sword suit which we have noted as being unfortunate, is not so here; the intimation is that success will be achieved after the expenditure of some effort, and that is hardly a misfortune.

The colors assigned to Tiphareth are: in Atziluth, a clear rose pink; in Briah, yellow; in Yetzirah, rich salmon pink; and in Assiah, golden amber. A prismatic mixture of these colors would closely approximate the color known in Sanskrit as *gerua*, the hue worn by the sannyasins (monks) of India, particularly those of the Ramakrishna Order.

NETZACH (Nun, Tzaddi, Cheth)

Before taking up the consideration of Netzach, it is necessary to say a few words of clarification. We have spoken throughout this book of the "Higher" and "Lower" Sephiroth, but it must be made clear and always born in mind that all the Sephiroth are equally holy. The Sephiroth are not located in the spatial world and they are not objects. They are symbols of states of mind and levels of consciousness, a map, so to speak, of the celestial forces in man and the universe. When we see a dot on a map, we do not think that it is a real city, inhabited by people, but only the representation of a city, which is something quite other than a dot. "Higher" and "Lower" refer only to situations upon the Otz Chiim, which is itself only a pictograph representing reality. A Sephirah might represent a material level of creation, but it is still spiritual. If this is not understood, all our studies on the Tree will prove fruitless.

Netzach, Victory, is the Seventh Sephirah, residing at the base of the Column of Compassion, below Chesed. Since its planetary sphere tells us much of that which is to be learned about Netzach, we shall first turn to that. It is Nogah, Venus, whose principal influence is reflected in the emotions and instincts of man. But Venus, or Aphrodite, is not Demeter, the goddess of Fertility; she is the goddess of love, and love is not only the relationship between the sexes, but more, including every sort of love, mother for child, friend for friend; brother for sister.

The worship of Aphrodite in Greece was more than a mere sexual orgy, although it had, at times, an orgiastic facet. Basically, it dramatized the polarity of energy and matter, the masculine and feminine principles, and the interaction of the two, each upon the other. On the human level, each of the sexes creates desire in the other; on the plane of the macrocosm, each of the qualities, energy and matter, responds to the other, energy entering into the material state through the fusion of atoms, and matter turning into energy through fission.

Sex is but one phase of polarity, the interaction of the pairs of opposites. Without polarity, the interplay of forces between Chokmah and Binah, Chesed and Geburah, or in the present case, Netzach and Hod, there would be no manifestation. The polarity of sex brings about increased manifestation on the mundane level; no birth being possible without both father and mother.

Another way of considering this polarity is in the field of electricity, the positive and negative charges being required to form a circuit. Hook up only the positive pole in your automobile battery and step on the starter. For all the good that it does, you might as well have disconnected the battery entirely. The same holds true, of course, for the negative pole. It takes both to make the current flow; and it takes both, the male and female aspects, the creative and receptive, to breathe life into manifestation, to cause manifestation to occur at all.

Again, Netzach must be studied in conjunction with its opposite number, Hod, the intellect. The two also represent the concrete functions of the one mind. Venus personifies the emotions, imagination and a certain irresponsibility; while Mercury, personifies stability, practicality and steadfastness. The emotions can lead to all sorts of difficulties if not balanced by a stabilizing force, but stability, unrelieved by emotion, produces nothing but a stodgy dullness. No significant work may be accomplished unless the element of imagination is present; however, unless the imagination is somewhat curbed by practical consideration, the result will be a Rube Goldberg sort of contraption. It took great imagination to plan for space travel; in fact, until a few years ago, space travel was confined entirely to the realm of science fiction. However, without the practical scientists, and their one-millionth of an inch tolerances, the moon rockets could not have been built.

The magical image of Netzach is a beautiful naked woman. Are we than to say that, perhaps, the sphere of Aphrodite is not seen to be actually one of sexual love? In answer, it can only be said that "to the pure, all things are pure." How does one react when shown a beautiful nude painting in an art gallery? Will he at once be filled with prurient thoughts? or will he observe it for what the artist intended it to be, a beautiful work of art? Can we meditate upon the magical image of a beautiful naked woman as a clue to the nature of Netzach, or will we let our minds roam into thoughts of lust? And, before all else, can we imagine the ancient patriarchs and rabbi presenting us with such an image if they had thought it prurient?

The text in the Sepher Yetzirah says of Netzach: "The Seventh Path is called the Occult Intelligence because of the brilliance of its intellectual powers, seen with the eye of the intellect and in concentration of faith." In the meditation upon the Higher Sephiroth, we have not employed the intellect, but the intuition. We have been dealing with the abstract, that which is beyond comprehension by the senses, the non-material aspects of manifestation. Now we are called upon to make use of the intellect, for we have come to the concrete world, and its symbols are also concrete.

These symbols are: the lamp, the girdle and the rose. The lamp represents the element of Fire, and gives a clue to the bond between Geburah, Mars, and Netzach, Venus; Mars, the fiery god of war, and Venus, the equally fiery goddess of love. The precipitation of essences by Geburah, passing through Tiphareth, descends upon Netzach. The girdle of Venus is part of mythological lore. It was made for her by her husband Vulcan, but when she wantoned with Mars, it fell off. The wearer of the girdle must remain chaste or else lose it. It is, therefore, a symbol of the faithful wife. The rose has ever been a symbol of love and, in fact, was considered as a potent ingredient in early love philters.

The Spiritual Experience of Netzach is the Vision of Beauty Triumphant, the result of a proper contemplation of the image of the beautiful naked Venus. This, in turn, creates within the heart of the aspirant the virtue of unselfishness, the love based not on self-satisfaction, but on performing acts of kindness. It should be needless to add that an improper contemplation of the image leads to lust.

The Divine Name given to Netzach in the World of Atziluth is Jehovah Tzabaoth, the Lord God of Hosts, a term frequently used in the Bible. It is to be remembered that the different names of God used in the Bible are not mere literary devices for avoiding excessive repetition, but indicate the level of consciousness governing that particular passage.

The Archangel of Netzach in the World of Briah is Haniel, who presides over the Angelic Host in the World of Yetzirah, the Elohim, or Gods, the rulers of nature. These are more in the order of nature spirits than of what we have come to consider Gods. We have already discussed the planetary sphere of Netzach in the World of Assiah: Nogah, or Venus.

The Sevens of the Tarot cards are assigned to Netzach: In Atziluth, the Seven of Wands is the Lord of Valor; in Briah, the Seven of Cups is the Lord of Illusory Success; in Yetzirah, the Seven of Swords is the Lord of Inconstant Effort; and in Assiah, the Seven of Pentacles is the Lord of Unrealized Success. Now that we have arrived at the Earth plane, it might be well to simplify the Four Worlds of the Kabbalah. In descending order, they are: the spiritual, mental, astral and physical levels.

Wands, the element of Fire, is a phallic symbol, and is also the suit of the spiritual level. Here, a spiritualized symbol of the phallus in combination with Venus, produces the concept of Valor. Cups, the element of Water, is a yoni symbol, and is the suit on the mental level. The doubling of femininity, the yoni and Venus, lacking the stabilizing effects of the masculine, produces Illusory Success. Swords, the element of Air, and a symbol of disruption, is a suit on the astral level. The feminine principle combined with disruption, leads to Inconstant Effort. Pentacles, is the element of Earth, and a symbol of actual conditions. On any level below the spiritual, Venus is somewhat less than stable and reliable; hence, the reading of the Seven of Pentacles as Unrealized Success.

The colors assigned to Netzach are: in Atziluth, amber; in Briah, emerald green; in Yetzirah, bright yellowish green; and in Assiah, olive with gold flecks.

HOD (He, Vau, Daleth)

Hod, Glory, is the Eighth Sephirah, residing at the base of the Column of Austerity, below Geburah. We have now come to the last—and lowest on the Tree—of the pairs of opposite Sephiroth and Netzach and Hod, the intuitive and pragmatic forces in the Astral-Physical plane. True to its position on the Column of Austerity, it is the essence of form, as Netzach is the essence of force.

This might be a good point at which to pause while notice is taken of something that perhaps should have been said earlier concerning the Gods and Goddesses with whom we have been dealing. It is to be hoped that the reader will have taken heed at what was said in a previous chapter about the reality of these Deities, but in case this has been overlooked or forgotten, let us discuss the matter briefly.

One might well ask, "Do the Gods and Goddesses really exist?" And a simple "yes" or "no" answer will not suffice. If by "really exist," one means to ask if they are members of a Heavenly Host that came into being with the beginning of creation, the answer is most certainly "no."

Primitive man came to associate all natural forces with an unseen intelligence. He did not ask the question: "Why is the wind blowing?" but "Who is causing the wind to blow?" As an exercise in primeval reasoning, this is not too bad. Poor old Neanderthal Man knew nothing of atmospheric pressures, cold fronts and warm fronts, and he reasoned that there must be a cause for all natural phenomena. Ergo, there is a being, such as themselves, only greater and invisible, who rules the wind. There is also one for rain, thunder, lightening, heat and cold. Somebody had to be operating the Sun, making it go across the sky each day, and putting its fire out at night.

These deities were rather crude in concept, but they became more and more refined. Let us not assume too lofty a position from which to look down on these savages. Remember the Third Chapter of Genesis which tells us that "they heard the voice of the Lord God walking in the garden in the cool of the day." Does this Lord God, who "walks" in the garden "in the cool of the day," bear much resemblance to the God of a more civilized people later in the Bible? There were, of course, many authors of the Bible, and they wrote at different stages of Hebraic history, so the God who enjoyed relief from the day's heat, became the wrathful God of vengeance, and then a just God, and finally a merciful Heavenly Father.

The primitive Gods and Goddesses were given names, and the people clothed them in forms, arrayed them in suitable robes, gave them weapons, orbs, scepters and other appropriate regalia, paired them off into married couples, and told each other stories about them, the legends that have come down to us. Some of these Deities had heads of animals to signify certain characteristics, and others had two, three and even four pairs of arms. And, of course, they all had powers, and those who have powers must be propitiated so that the powers will be used in ways favorable to the one propitiating them.

Which brings us back to our question: "Do the Gods and Goddesses really exist?" The answer of the occultist is a most resounding "yes." But there is a qualification to be added: they exist as the creation of man; the creature has created them in his own likeness, and the combined belief of millions of humans, and more than belief, the worship of those humans, has given a certain substance to the Deities.

So there is a warlike Mars, an amorous Venus, a disciplinarian Saturn, and a Lord of Heaven Jupiter, and these will continue to exist as long as they are worshipped and invoked. There is a Brahma who creates the universe at the beginning of each cycle, a Vishnu to preserve it during that cycle, and a Siva to preside at its dissolution. According to Hindu cosmology, when the world is to be created anew, Brahma awakes from his long sleep of 4,320,000,000 years, called "the Night of Brahma," and must first come to realize who he is. Only then can he set about his creative activities. Is this not a way of saying that the people, feeling the need of having an explanation of the reason for the existence of the physical universe, finally arrived at this legend; in other words, that it is they, the people themselves, who create Brahma, and that Brahma exists because of them?

Once the people have created their Gods and sustained them by belief and worship, propitiating them by offerings and sacrifice, and serving them in those ways that have become traditional, the Gods become the servants of the people. That is to say, that although the Gods may seem to be the masters, having been clothed in more than regal power and splendor, part of their power has been granted to them for the express purpose of using it to help the people. And, in the long run, as it must to all Gods, comes a long and lingering twilight and, finally, death, for the people are fickle, and new

Gods are created to serve them. Once the God ceases to be sustained, he fades away into that limbo which is the graveyard for the multitude of forgotten Deities.

This should not be too shocking a concept; we do the same thing in our dreams. We suddenly find ourselves chased by an ogre, a tiger, or other menacing figure. We fear him and flee. To us, he is very real and most terrifying. And then we awake and there is no ogre. Who is this ogre? He is the creation of our own minds; we created him and sustain him by believing in him. He frightens us, and yet, he is our servant, his every act the result of our own mental processes. But as long as we believe in him, he seems to be our master, and will continue as such until we awaken. But when we do awake, the ogre is gone and soon, let us hope, forgotten. However, can we say with any degree of certainty, that the ogre never existed? If not, then what was our dream all about? He did exist, if only in our minds; he was real, if only for a time; he was our master, if only because we endowed him with his powers.

And so it is with the Gods and Goddesses, we make them and break them, and the universe is littered with their memories. For the occultist, they serve as very useful tools, keys with which to unlock the doors to the various levels of consciousness. Meditating on Venus, we first enter into the sphere of love, both personal and impersonal; on Mars, courage, and so on throughout the Heavenly Heirarchy. Following this method smoothes our path to the heights, a path which is sufficiently rugged and irregular to suit the hardiest taste at best.

And so to return to Hod: the text in the *Sepher Yetzirah* says, "The Eighth Path is called the Ideal or Perfect Intelligence, because it is the mean of the primal power, having no root to which it may adhere and rest, save in the hidden recesses of Gedulah [Chesed], out of which is precipitated its true essence." The primal power is composed of force and form, and Hod is said to be the "mean" of these, that is, the mid-point between them. Hod is a reflection across the Tree of Chesed. As with all reflections, things are reversed, and that of Chesed, which emanates force, is reflected in Hod, which receives the force and formulates it.

This concept is further carried out by the Magical Image assigned to Hod, that of an hermaphrodite, the dual male-female image. Most ancient religions of which we have any record had their Hermaphrodite Deities; Quetzalcoatl, in Mexico; Ardanari Iswara, in India; and Hermaphroditus, son of Hermes and Aphrodite, in Greece, as well as others in Egypt, China and Persia. Mercury, the Deity of our present Sephirah, is considered by the alchemists as an hermaphrodite, being depicted as a two-headed figure, frequently accompanied by the word *Rebis,* or "double thing." There is a clear indication that the early Jews regarded Adam as an hermaphrodite, as shown in Genesis 1:27: "So God created man in his own image; male and female created he them." Since Eve had not yet been made out of Adam's rib, the "them" who were male and female could only have been the First Man.

The Divine Name assigned to Hod in the World of Atziluth is Elohim Tzabaoth, the God of Hosts. Again, it is to be noted that Elohim is a mixed masculine-feminine name, and that the three Sephiroth on the right hand Column of Austerity have Elohim in their Names. This further carries out the Image of the Hermaphrodite.

The Archangel of Hod in the World of Briah is Michael, the mighty warrior. In Revelations 12:7-8, we read, "And there was war in heaven: Michael and his angels fought against the dragon; and the dragon fought his angels, and prevailed not." Michael is nearly always depicted as treading on a serpent and impaling it with his sword. He frequently holds a balance scale in his hand, showing the equilibrium that is expressed in the text of the *Sepher Yetzirah:* "it is the mean of the primal power." The serpent is, of course, a phallic symbol, a symbol of inhibited sex; but here it is held in check by the balancing grace of Hod. The serpent still lives, but is controlled; sex is not to be killed, but expended with some discretion, as something more than mere animalism.

The Host of Angels assigned to Hod in the World of Yetzirah is the Beni Elohim, Sons of Gods, those who do the work of God.

The planetary sphere of Hod in the World of Assiah is, as we have seen, Mercury, the Hermes of the Greeks, having a common derivation with "hermaphrodite," and Thoth of the Egyptians. The Hebrew name for Mercury is Kokab.

The Spiritual Experience of Hod is the Vision of Splendor. Hod, which means Glory, would certainly be visualized as Splendor, and he who has this vision realizes the splendor of the created universe and becomes the master of equilibrium and universal order.

The Symbols of Hod are the Sacred Names, the Versicles and the Apron. The Sacred Names are those Names of Divinity by which the magician invokes the powers of the universe. These names are not like those of humans or places, built up out of very simple meanings, or no meanings at all, but mere sounds. They are complex formulae resulting from mathematical calculations based upon the numerical equivalents of the letters. One such Kabbalistic use of the formula was that of the Mark of the Beast, in Revelations, which is revealed in this fashion: "Here is wisdom. Let him that hath understanding count the number of the Beast: for it is the number of a man; and his number is Six hundred threescore and six." He "that hath understanding," that is he who knows the formula, will be able to work this out quite easily as spelling out "Neron Caesar," Neron being the Greek name for Nero. Who is the Beast, the arch-enemy of the young Christian faith, who "opened his mouth in blasphemy against God," and under whose rule "no man might buy or sell, save he that had the mark, or the name of the beast, or the number of his name," which probably refers to coins? Why, my fellow occultists, I don't want to speak the dreaded name for fear someone will report me and I will be taken to the arena to be eaten by lions. But I will tell you his number and you can figure it our for yourselves. It is 666.

The Versicles are short verses, what the Hindus call *mantras*. They contain a sacred name of either an aspect of God or an avatar, and are to be repeated constantly as a way to achieve the vision of that aspect or avatar.

The Apron is a familiar symbol of the Freemasons, who wear it as a garment appropriate to their order's name. A mason is a builder, one who constructs in form, and this apron symbol is, therefore, a most ancient one, used in the Mysteries since the time of Solomon. Hod stands as not only the maker of forms, but the maker of magical forms, the initiate's sphere of formal magic.

The Eights of the Tarot cards have been assigned to Hod: in Atziluth, the Eight of Wands is the Lord of Celerity; in Briah, the Eight of Cups is the Lord of Forsaken Success; in Yetzirah, the Eight of Swords is the Lord of Limited Energy; and in Assiah, the Eight of Pentacles is the Lord of Caution. The three lower suits are all negative and inhibiting, but inhibitions are required to check the Venus forces that would otherwise run rampant. Only on the spiritual level is there the freedom of Celerity.

The colors assigned to Hod are: in Atziluth, purple violet; in Briah, orange; in Yetzirah, russet red; and in Assiah, a yellow-tinged black with white flecks.

YESOD (Yod, Samech, Vau, Daleth)

Yesod, the Foundation, is the Ninth Sephirah, residing on the central Column below Tiphareth. Once more, as in the Second Triangle, force and form have resulted in equilibrium; Netzach and Hod have come to rest in Yesod.

But Yesod is more than just the point of balance between force and form. Each Sephirah also receives emanations from the one above it on its Column, and this means that Yesod receives an outpouring from Tiphareth, and thus also from Kether. The precipitations Yesod receives from Hod are also from Binah, through Geburah; those it receives from Netzach have come down from Chokmah through Chesed. So, all the precipitations have come down to Yesod from all eight of the Sephiroth above. For this reason, the Kabbalists have called Yesod the "Receptacle of the Precipitations."

Therefore, we have the text in the *Sepher Yetzirah*, which says of Yesod: "The Ninth Path is called the Immaculate Intelligence, because it sanctifies the Precipitations. It verifies and rectifies the plan of their representations, and orders the unity in which they are planned without decreasing or dividing it."

It is necessary to bear this text in mind as we study the symbolism of Yesod, for we are going to find some strange contradictions. For the most part, we see symbols of strength, the Magical Image of Yesod, for instance, is that of a beautiful naked man, very strong. One would suspect that this might have some reference to Atlas, who is certainly a foundation, carrying the world on his mighty shoulders. But then we find that the Planetary Sphere of Yesod is Levanah, the Moon, that most changeable orb. Shakespeare said it very well:

> ROMEO: Lady, by yonder moon I swear
> That tips with silver all these fruit-free tops—
> JULIET: O! swear not by the moon, the
>   inconstant moon,
> That monthly changes in her circled orb,
> Lest that thy love prove likewise variable.

The Moon is anything but a model of strength, and is of an aqueous nature. Her ruler is Gabriel, the Archangel of the element of Water.

How are we to bring these conflicting concepts into harmony, for harmonize them we must, since there can be no discord on the Tree? Here we have strength on the one hand, and the weakness of water on the other. The harmonization is provided in the Yetziratic text, which tells us that Yesod "orders the unity in which they (the precipitations) are planned," this planning having taken place in Hod. The formless force of Netzach, which can be likened to water, and the formative force of Hod, have become unified in the way in which they were planned, by Yesod.

Yesod performs another very important function, that of "sanctifying the precipitations," all of which are to pass down into Malkuth, the physical plane. "It verifies and rectifies the plan," that is, Yesod supervises the plan for the dense physical plane in which matter is to hold sway.

The Ninth Sephirah is, then, the plane of the *Akasha*, the all-pervading etheric substance out of which matter is formed. We shall return again to the Four Elements which form the sphere of Malkuth. There is also a fifth element, which we will call by its Hindu name, *Akasha*, since its Western equivalent, ether, is apt to be confusing. Scientists have debated the question of the ether, the subtle substance that interpenetrates the physical universe, and have finally come to an apparent agreement, although they are not unanimous in this, that the ether does not exist. It is not with their concept of ether that we are concerned, but with the even more subtle concept of the Akasha. It is all well and good to speak of the four elements as the building blocks of matter, but what force brought them into being? Will it be the idea that God somehow created these components of matter out of himself? That may be a little more advanced than an idea of God, sitting on his throne in Heaven, commanding matter to exist, but it still does not go far enough. Most occultists and mystics agree that there is more to it than that. But what?

Nothing can be defined in terms of itself. This process would be like trying to define "love" in terms of itself: love is love. We still do not know any more than we did before. It does not help much to define one term by its simile, in the manner of a dictionary at this author's side: Love is affection; affection is love. We must go outside all our terms to find true meaning. Thus, Fire, Water, Air and Earth cannot be defined in terms of each other, but they can be defined by a fifth term, the unmanifested Akasha.

According to the Kabbalah, God did not directly create matter, nor even Akasha, but the precipitations, from Kether to Hod, including the interaction of Netzach and Hod upon each other, result in the precipitation of the Yesodic Akasha. And Akasha, in turn, precipitates the four elements. Yesod, the sphere of Akasha, is also the sphere of Maya, for out of Maya is projected the universe.

Maya has been called the "Mother of the Universe," for a reason that becomes quite clear once it is understood. The ancient Rishis explained the existence of matter in a spiritual universe by neither denying or affirming the reality of matter. They said, in effect, that matter was real, but that we did not see it for what it was because we can only cognate it through the senses, and the senses are poor tools at best. Our eyes do not see more than the shadows of things, and even these shadows are only seen by reflected light. When we see something that we think is red, we are only seeing a ray of light reflected from its surface, out of which all color has been filtered except that of red. The object, then, has every color but red, and is not actually red at all. And, of course, we only see the surface of things. When we think we know someone because we are looking at him, we are only seeing his outer layer, and that is but a miniscule fraction of the person.

The above deals only with our limited and faulty vision of an object. To know that object, we would have to see it as it really is, the thing in itself. This we cannot do in our mundane state, and so we are not aware that there is anything more to it than its outer appearance. If we could know the thing in itself, we would see it as not really material, but a galaxy of dancing electrons and protons that are not in the realm of what we refer to as material; rather are they pure energy, and therefore, without that solidity we have come to attribute to matter. The man of illumination does see matter in this, or at least a similar, way. We cannot know exactly what it is he sees, for he could not describe it to us, even if there were the words by which to do so. It is said that his eyes are opened, and he knows the truth of all things. He has pierced the veil of Maya; he has gone beyond Yesod.

There is an additional function attributed to Akasha,

that of connecting mind to matter; the perception of sensations, through the nerves and skin, conducted to the brain, can be charted and understood, but the connection between the brain and consiousness cannot be explained in terms of material brain and immaterial consciousness. Only when we postulate an intervening medium, Akasha, can we comprehend the underlying basis, the foundation, of this process. And that is the name of the Sephirah: Yesod, the Foundation.

The Divine Name assigned to Yesod in the World of Atziluth is Shaddai el Chai, the Almighty Living God. This is the Divine Force that influences the Moon, and is said to be the cause of increase and decrease, as in the waxing and waning of the tides. We all know that the tides are caused by the gravitational pull of the Moon, but just what, exactly, is meant by "gravitational pull"? Science can no more define "gravitation" than it can "electricity." The Kabbalistic explanation of gravity as the action of Shaddai el Chai is at least as valid as the non-explanation of science.

The Archangel assigned to Yesod in the World of Briah is Gabriel. Longfellow again gives us a view of Gabriel that shows his understanding of the Archangel's attributes:

> I am the angel of the moon . . .
> Nearest the earth, it is my ray
> That best illumines the midnight way.
> I bring the gift of *hope*.

The Angelic Host assigned to Yesod in the World of Yetzirah is the Kerubim, the Strong Ones. This order is frequently mentioned in the Bible, and is first encountered in the Third Chapter of Genesis: ". . . and he placed at the east of the garden of Eden Cherubims. . . ."

The planetary sphere assigned to Yesod in the World of Assiah is, as has already been mentioned, Levanah, the Moon. The Goddess of the Moon is called by various names, the Roman Diana or Luna; the Greek

Artemis, Selene, or Hecate. The Goddess is sometimes considered as the most chaste of the Goddesses, not a difficult pinnacle to achieve, if we are to believe mythology, but at Ephesus, in the Great Temple of Artemis, which was one of the ancient Seven Wonders of the World, the Goddess was represented by a statue of a woman having many breasts, and was thus held to be a fertility symbol.

The Spiritual Experience of Yesod is a Vision of Machinery of the Universe. It cannot be said too many times that a vision, such as those for each Sephirah, is more than a mere "seeing" of something; it is a total experience of that level of consciousness, culminating in the vision of Kether, Union with God. The Vision, or knowledge, of the Machinery of the Universe, is the knowledge of the way in which the universe operates.

The Symbols assigned to Yesod are the Perfume and the Sandals. Perfume, or more correctly, incense, is an important adjunct in all ceremonial religion, and this would include magic. When one enters a church in which incense is burning, his mood is made to change very quickly from whatever worldly thoughts he may have had to those of more spiritual matters. Incense sets the mood, and since its effect is to raise the material to the ethereal, or from Malkuth to Yesod, it is an appropriate symbol for the Ninth Sephirah.

The Sandals are also of significance, particularly in magical rites. It is said that the magnetic forces of the earth are assimilated through the feet, and the magician does not want to block these out by wearing thick-soled shoes. When Moses saw the burning bush, and God called to him: "Moses, Moses." Moses replied, "Here am I." And God said, "Draw not nigh hither: put off thy shoes from off thy feet, for the place whereon thou standest is holy ground." The magician, wanting to stand on holy ground, dons sandals that have been dedicated to this one purpose and no other.

The Nines of the Tarot cards have been assigned to Yesod: in Atziluth, the Nine of Wands is the Lord of Great Strength; in Briah, the Nine of Cups is the Lord of

Material Happiness; in Yetzirah, the Nine of Swords is the Lord of Despair and Cruelty; and in Assiah, the Nine of Pentacles is the Lord of Material Gain. Except for the Sword suit, these are the goals of the magician working on the plane of Yesod. Only he who does not work in the proper manner in this sphere will descend to despair and act in a cruel manner.

The colors assigned to Yesod are: in Atziluth, indigo; in Briah, violet; in Yetzirah, purple verging on black; in Assiah, lemon yellow, with azure flecks.

MALKUTH (Mem, Lamed, Kaph, Vau, Tau)

Malkuth, the Kingdom, is the Tenth Sephirah, residing on the lowest point on the Column of Serenity, below Yesod. It alone is not a part of any Triangle, and is not precipitated by the pairs of opposites coming into equilibrium, but as the nadir in the scheme of creation, it receives the influences of all the higher Sephiroth. It is not only the low point on the Tree of Life, but the turning point, since all the forces that have flowed down into it must begin the slow climb back up the path to the source from which they came.

The stability of Malkuth is expressed in the fact that it is the only Sephirah in a state of equilibrium that has been precipitated by a sphere in a similar state. Were it not so, the earth plane and all those who dwell upon it could not exist in stable material form. The Sephiroth above it on the central Column have been described as in a state of equilibrium, but it has been an equilibrium between action and reaction, not a stability in mani-festation of form. Malkuth gives us the stability of inertia; things remain as they are, at least for a time. We are able to recognize those we know because they do not change radically from day to day.

Malkuth has but one neighbor on the Tree by which one can consider its relationships, and that is Yesod. We might make the comparison of the sculptor and his clay, each of whom relies upon the other for significance. The sculptor would have nothing upon which to work were it not for the clay, and the clay would remain a shapeless mass were it not for the sculptor. Yesod would have no outlet for its formative powers were it not able to manifest them in Malkuth. Yesod is the sphere of form, but these are the forms of the Will o' the Wisp, changing more swiftly than the eye—a proverbial eye—can follow. Yesod is the former of things; Malkuth is that which has been formed.

Malkuth is the visible form of the forces precipitated by Yesod, and all living things in Malkuth receive their life forces from the Ninth Sephirah. But Yesod does not work directly on matter, since atoms are quite recalcitrant and resist force outside themselves. Therefore, Yesod must work to influence the subtle elements, beginning with Fire, after which the other elements fall into line and, through them, the material particles themselves.

In spite of all that has been said earlier to the effect that all of the Sephiroth are equally holy, one is still apt to think of Malkuth as materialistic and unspiritual. But Malkuth is not the lowest point of evolution, the bottom of the barrel of life. It should be considered as a pylon in an air race, around which the airplanes must go before they can turn for the finish line. And that pylon must be rounded, or the pilot is disqualified. We must spend the necessary time in the material sphere, learning the lessons it has to teach us. To attempt to escape from it before we have mastered the physical plane is impossible; the one who tries will only have to go back and start again. There is no cheating in this race. It is not that some Deity will disqualify him; he will disqualify himself, because he had not the basic knowledge required before he can take the next step. The chief reason that the kindergarten graduate is not permitted to enter college is that he would not be able to comprehend the work, or possibly even to read his assignments. The path must be negotiated step by step. It may seem unromantic and dull, not at all what the fast-buck gurus teach, but all that the fast-buck gurus accomplish is the gathering of a quantity of fast bucks; their deluded disciples remain deluded, and will in all likelihood go in search of an even less qualified—but even more glib—spinner of promises and dreams.

Mankind, since the beginning of civilization, has worked in the sphere of Malkuth, and that work has been most productive in terms of art, music, literature and science. We live not only a better life, but a richer and fuller life, than did our barbarian ancestors. Those who would return to the primitive life with Jean Jacques Rousseau, must be prepared to live without medicine or hygiene, without electricity or indoor plumbing, without any of the ameliorating features of our lives. They must also be prepared to suffer from toothache, famine, and the depredations of wild animals. One does not turn his back on civilization and all its works, but one can master the essence of Malkuth and begin his climb to the top.

The Magical Image of Malkuth is a young woman, enthroned, crowned and veiled. Who is this young woman? A statue of her is mentioned by Proclus, the Neo-Platonist, who lived during most of the fifth century. On its base was this inscription;

> I am that which is,
> Has been, and shall be.
> My veil no one has lifted.
> The fruit I bore was the Sun.

She is, of course, Isis, the veiled Queen of the Moon, whose husband was Osiris, God of the Sun, and whose child (the fruit I bore) was Horus, also a God of the Sun. Her veil is a symbol of the mystery, and it has been lifted, but the sculptor, perhaps, was not aware of this. The veil does not symbolize an insoluble mystery, but only the fact that her outer form conceals the inner spiritual forces.

The text in the *Sepher Yetzirah* says of Malkuth: "The Tenth Path is called the Effulgent Intelligence because it is glorified above all heads and sits upon the

Throne of Binah. It illuminates the radiance of every light, and causes an influence to flow down from the Prince of Countenances, the Archangel of Kether." It is clear from this that Malkuth is, among other aspects, Binah operating on a more material level. Here we have the composite Aphrodite-Ceres and the Egyptian Isis-Hathor, the combination of *agape* and *eros,* sacred and profane love. The word "profane" is used in its sense of "worldly," or "unconsecrated," rather than having the meaning of "irreligious." Aphrodite gives the stimulus, but it is Malkuth who is motivated, to become Ceres, the fertile Mother on the physical plane.

A light may shine, but nothing is illumined until the light is reflected by matter. An astronaut, standing on the Moon, can see the Sun and the surface beneath him, but he cannot see the sky, because it is black. Seen from Earth, the sky appears blue, because the dust particles in the atmosphere reflect the light. Therefore, Malkuth "illuminates the radiance of every light." This explains the next phrase in the text: "and causes an influence to flow down from the Prince of Countenances, the Arch-angel of Kether." As light is made visible by reflection from material objects, so is the influence of Metatron, the Archangel of Kether, made operative in the physical universe by its reflection in Malkuth. Malkuth is, in a very real sense, the *raison d'etre* of not only Kether, but the Otz Chiim itself.

Titles assigned to Malkuth are more numerous than those of any other Sephirah: The Gate, the Gate of Death, the Gate of the Shadow of Death, the Gate of Tears, the Gate of Justice, the Gate of Prayer, the Gate of the Daughter of the Mighty Ones, the Gate of the Garden of Eden, the Inferior Mother, the Virgin. Also, Malkah, the Queen, as has been previously mentioned, and Kallah, the Bride.

Most of these have to do with the idea of a gate, and this is most suitable. The Gate is, of course, a yoni symbol, signifying here the entrance into physical life. We have already seen that the gate of creation, which is the Gate of the Garden of Eden, is also the Gate of

Death, as well as the Gate of the Shadow of Death and the Gate of Tears. All of this was discussed under the Sephirah Geburah and needs no further elucidation here.

The title of the Gate of Justice is appropriate, since all that occurs, according to the mystics and occultists, is just. One may be treated unjustly, as almost everyone has been at one time or another, but this is justice, being the result of karmas made either in this or a past life. Of course, the one committing the injustice has laid up an unpleasant slice of karma for himself.

We have seen that Tiphareth has as one of its titles Melekh, the King. Now we see that Malkuth is Malkah, the Queen, which is Kallah, the Bride. Melekh reaches across the Veil of the Temple into the material world, the Son of the Heavenly Father fecundating the Earth Mother, the last stage of creation.

The Divine Names assigned to Malkuth are two: Adonai Malekh, the Lord Who Is King, and Adonai ha Aretz, the Lord of Earth. These titles could well be combined into one, The Lord King of Earth. This is God manifested in nature, and is, therefore, the aspect of God worshipped in the Mysteries of Isis and of Dionysus, which were nature cults.

The Archangel of Malkuth is Sandalphon, the Dark Angel, in contrast to Metatron, the Bright Angel. He is said to receive the prayers of the faithful, which he weaves into crowns. As Longfellow put it:

> And he gathers the prayers as he stands,
> And they change into flowers in his hands,
> Into garlands of purple and red.

Sandalphon's position is that of the Lord of Karma, and his rule over Malkuth is the reason for its title the Gate of Justice, as was discussed above.

The Host of Angels assigned to Malkuth are the Ashim, Souls of Fire. This name means the consciousness within the atom, for the atom is the fiery particle out of which all material things are built.

The Planetary Sphere of Malkuth is that of the Elements, which we have already discussed at some length.

The Spiritual Experience of Malkuth is the Vision of the Holy Guardian Angel. This is the individual guardian of each human being, and is actually our own higher selves, indwelling us during an incarnation, and after death, become the nucleus around which out next lives are formed. This is the first of the three most important visions, the Vision of our own true natures, the second being the vision of Tiphareth, the Son of God, and the third being the vision of Kether, in which one has Union with God.

The Symbols assigned to Malkuth are: the Double Cube, the Magic Circle, the Triangle, and the Simple, or Equal-armed Cross. The Double Cube represents the concept of the macrocosm and the microcosm, Heaven and Earth, Spirit and Matter. It is best expressed in the Emerald Tablets of Thoth, the Egyptian God of Wisdom, called by the Greeks Hermes Trismegistus, the "thrice greatest Hermes": "As above, so below." The Magic Circle is the figure drawn by magicians, the "Holy Ground" corresponding to the words in God's injunction to Moses from the burning bush. The Double Cube becomes an altar in the center of the Magic Circle.

The Triangle, with its apex uppermost, symbolizes the Element of Fire, and the aspirations of mankind toward Union with God, the urge to rise from the base, signifying material existence, to the point, which is the origin of all and the place where matter ceases to exist in any form.

The Equal-armed Cross symbolizes the relationship of Heaven and Earth, the upright signifying the Celestial, and the cross-piece the mundane. It also denotes the conjunction of the pairs of opposites, the spiritual and the material, and thus has long stood as a symbol of agony in the original meaning of that word (Greek: *agon*, a contest, a struggle). The spiritual path is a struggle, and one that is painful on occasion. The agony of Christ refers not only to His physical suffering, but to the struggle within Himself, not only on the Cross, but throughout the whole of His ministry.

The Cross represents an entirely different concept as well, symbolizing the Four Elements, the Planetary Sphere of Malkuth. It signifies the ideal of equilibrium of the Elements in Malkuth, which, when achieved, gives the perfect vision of the Tenth Sephirah.

The Tens of the Tarot cards have been assigned to Malkuth: in Atziluth, the Ten of Wands is the Lord of Oppression; in Briah, the Ten of Cups is the Lord of Perfected Success; in Yetzirah, the Ten of Swords is the Lord of Ruin; and in Assiah, the Ten of Pentacles is the Lord of Wealth.

The colors assigned to Malkuth are: in Atziluth, yellow; in Briah, olive; in Yetzirah, russet; and in Assiah, black, with yellow rays. These are depicted as the colors of the spaces between the arms of the Cross positioned similarly to the St. Andrew's Cross, which looks like the letter "X" and symbolizes the juncture of Heaven and Earth. The upper space, pointing toward Yesod, is yellow; the space to the right, towards Netzach, is olive; that to the left, towards Hod, is russet; and that at the bottom, towards the Qliphoth, is black. These colors represent those of the Sephiroth at the heads of the three Columns: the pure white brilliance of Kether, the pure soft blue of Chokmah, and the crimson of Binah have been dulled down to yellow, olive and russet by the materiality of Earth.

CHAPTER 9

THE QLIPHOTH

WE ARE NOT going to deal with the Qliphoth in anything like the detail that we have given to our study of the Sephiroth, and the reason is very simple: we are treading on dangerous ground. Only the most accomplished magician may avail himself of these powers without destroying himself.

Such a magician was Abramelin the Magus, an Egyptian of the fourteenth century, whose system of magic is the most effective and potent known. It was transmitted to his pupil Abraham, who transcribed it and produced the manuscript now in the archives of the *Bibliotheque de l'Arsenal*, Paris, *The Book of the Sacred Magic of Abra-Melin, as Delivered by Abraham the Jew unto His Son Lamech.* According to Abramelin, the magician goes through an extended ceremony of preliminary purification, and then invokes the demonic, as well as the angelic forces.

Abramelin employed the Gematria, an intricate system of cosmic numerology, out of which certain truths may be learned and certain powers invoked by using the numerical valves of the Letters composing the Divine Names. Out of his vast experience he was able to write portions of his book involved with such activities as "The Convocation of the Spirits," "The Classes of Veritable Magic," "Manner of Carrying Out the Operations," and even "How to be Beloved by a Woman."

The danger underlying the teachings of Abramelin is that of the danger in an unmarked bottle of poison. One has to take care to perform all of the processes prescribed by the Magus; to pick and choose among them is to court disaster. Since this is the case, we will not attempt to set forth his methods in view of the fact that nothing like the space required to explain them fully is available in this book. We will content ourselves with a brief coverage of the nature of the Qliphoth in order to complete our picture of the Tree of Life.

Kabbalists recognize two distinct elements: one can be thought of as an interior, life-giving aspect which manifests itself in a vital energy or Form. The other is, as Myer writes, "purely exterior, plastic, and material, which is considered inert and without vitality, always tending to dissolution and a return to its original atoms. These two are considered as existing in all the created, in a greater or less degree. The first as a symbol of Blessing and life, the latter as a symbol of Curse and death. The first is the Kabbalistic hierarchy of the angelic host and good spirits, the latter that of the demons or Qliphoth, *i.e.,* shells and evil spirits. The Deity has created the good and the evil, and one is absolutely necessary to the existence of the other. It considers that each human being is accompanied throughout its life on earth and is influenced spiritually by two spirits, the good and evil."

Myer describes Qliphoth as the mere shells or rinds of existence. They are thought of, he tells, as "energies or forces which are destructive and injurious to man. They, too, form Ten Degrees answering to the lowest extremity of the Ten Sephirothic emanative rays, and in these Ten lower degrees, darkness and impurity increase the further they are removed from the primordial source."

Two interesting quotes from the Zohar in relationship to the Qliphoth:

(1) "Above in the Tree of Life exist no strange Qliphoths for it is said: 'With Thee dwelleth no Evil' but in the Tree, Below, exist the strange Qliphoths. . . . Above are not any Qliphoth for no one can enter in the Gate of the King in a strange garment, but the Qliphoth are below."

(2) "The Qliphoth (i.e., Shells and Evil Spirits) will not depart till the time of the Day of Resurrection, when the dead revive from the grave, then shall the Qliphoth be broken and from the Brain inside, the light shall shine into the world."

For the occultist whose interest is solely that of raising his being to the highest possible level of consciousness, the Qliphoth are merely of passing interest, but to the one who would employ the Tree in the performance of magic, they are of a rank of importance second only to the Sephiroth themselves. In the process of invoking the forces of any Sephirah, its opposite Qliphah will sooner or later have to be taken into consideration. And he who deals with these must have purified himself to the extent that he may not only invoke the Sphere of Venus (Divine Love), but be able to prevent the forces of its Qliphah, Lust, to take him under its sway.

The Tree upon which the Ten Qliphoth are arrayed is not a separate Tree, but a mirror image of the Otz Chiim, the mirror being placed at the base in such a manner as to reflect the image downward. The Averse Tree, then, has its highest point below—and corresponding to—the Sephirah of Malkuth, and its lowest point is the reflection of Kether.

The individual Qliphah is not precisely the opposite of its corresponding Sephirah, but possesses its nature carried to an extreme. Thus Geburah, the Sphere of Mars, represents strength and severity, but its reverse, called the Burning and Conflicting Forces, goes beyond severity to brutality and sadism. And the Qliphah of Chesed is the extreme of mercy, being called the Tolerators of Destruction. How apt a name that is for describing so much of what troubles this land today.

Much of the present rioting, mugging, bombing and general street violence can be laid at the door of those who tolerate destruction no less than at the door of the criminals themselves.

These two Sephiroth and their corresponding Qliphoth demonstrate that evil need not always be the direct opposite of good, but may be merely an unreasonable extension of good. We know the old proverb: "Do even good in moderation." We know that while mankind must have food to live, too much food will kill. In like manner too much breath will result in hyperventilation; too much of sleep will dull the senses, and so on, *ad infinitum*. However, the fact that evil may be an extension of good carried to the extreme is only to be said of those Sephiroth residing in the right and left Columns of the Tree, the dynamic Sephiroth. It is somewhat otherwise with those on the Column of Serenity.

The Sephiroth in a state of equilibrium are static, and their corresponding Qliphoth are not extensions of the Sephirothic virtues into evil extremes, but rather are they evil in themselves. Thus Tiphareth is the Sphere of the Redeemer, the harmonizer of the opposing forces of Chesed and Geburah, and its reverse is the Sphere of Discord. As the Archangel of Tiphareth is Raphael, the Bringer of Light, so the angel of its Qliphah is Lucifer, the Light Bearer, an angel who fell from grace. Lucifer is not so much a force of positive evil as the mere absence of good. But is this not, perhaps, what evil really is? Evil is not a force in itself, but a force from which the good has been withdrawn. The two most evil men in modern history were, by all odds, Hitler and Stalin. They contained within themselves tremendous reservoirs of force, and if they had also contained reservoirs of the virtues, love, wisdom and charity, they might have done an inestimable amount of good. But good was apparently totally absent from their natures, and the result was the chaos of a great war and a sorely wounded world.

Too many followers of the world's great religions look upon the cosmic scheme as a war between the forces of good and the forces of evil, between construction and destruction, between light (spirituality) and darkness (materiality). But the true battle, if it can be called such, is that between knowledge and ignorance, and this is not a battle at all, since with the advent of knowledge, ignorance ceases. As Swami Prabhavananda has so well put it: "If you walk into a dark room, even if it has been dark for a thousand years, one lighted lamp will dispel the darkness at once." There can be no real conflict between light and darkness, for the darkness possesses no power by which to resist the light. The blackest night can only reign until the Sun is ready to rise. Evil can only reign until good is introduced. And evil does not retreat as a beaten foe from the arena; it merely vanishes into nothingness.

The reverse of the coin of Tiphareth, the Redeemer, are the Zourmiel, the Disputers, who have been called "the black titans who are ever opposed to each other." This concept is most significant in view of what has just been said. Even in the ranks of evil, the forces cannot co-operate, and we know that "a house divided against itself cannot stand." The Sephirah of Tiphareth works to bring all things into harmony; the Qliphah of Tiphareth works with equal diligence to destroy itself. This is rather good news for our side, the side of decency, humanity, peace and good will.

The forces of good have the upper hand and, come to think of it, this is the way it has to be; this is a fundamental imperative. Consider for a moment the alternative, that the forces of evil, the forces of destruction, were in the ascendant. We are dealing in impossibilities, since there could not be a universe based on destruction. Such a universe would be on the road to annihilation before it could even come into being. We do not have to take the goodness of God, that is, the constructive impulse of creation, on faith. Even so weak a weapon as reason must tell us that, while there are forces of destruction, they cannot withstand the forces of construction. Just take a look around; here is the world, and it has been constructed despite whatever destructive influences there may be. To put it in sporting terms: the struggle between God and the Devil is the greatest mismatch of all time. The Devil may win an occasional round, but he is steadily losing the fight.

Since we are not promulgating a system of magic, we need not go further into the Qliphoth. Our goal is that which stands at the end of the occult path up the Tree of Life, and if we tread that path with persistence, we will encounter few signs of the Qliphoth. Should one appear, that is, should we find ourselves leaning to an extreme expression of the spirit of the particular Sephirah under contemplation, it is a simple matter to invoke by prayer the Archangel of that sphere and beg his good offices in preserving us from the results arising out of our over-extension of the essence of that Sephirah.

Once again, let us make it clear that there are, in all probability, no such personages as Archangels. However, they have been created by the protracted belief and worship of countless devotees. They embody certain principles and virtues, certain attributes and concepts. It is, perhaps, easier to invoke the ideational Venus, than to have to think through all the things for which Venus stands.

Thus, if we are meditating upon Netzach (Venus), and we find our thoughts extending beyond love to its Qliphothic extreme, lust, one merely appeals to the Archangel Haniel for guidance. The feeling of lust is not defeated; it simply disappears. This is the profound meaning of the maxim based on Biblical quotations: "Resist not evil, but overcome evil with good."

At this point, the reader is likely to say, "All very neat and tidy. But didn't you lure me into this chapter with the warning of an irrevocable danger?"

The answer is: yes.

All right, then, what kind of danger? What can happen to a person who attempts to invoke or deal with Qliphoth? What are some of these "consequences," for instance, written about by Herbert Weiner in his book on the Kabbalah today, *9½ Mystics*?

Enough questions.

Consider Isaac Luria, a sixteenth century mystic who propounded Zohar studies and exercises. A staunchly conservative man, Luria attempted to cement the aspect of ritual, rabbinical ritual, by means of mystical practice. This evolved to a point where, in the morning prayer, the devotee, originally throwing himself on the ground before the Deity, went beyond that symbolism, and literally thought to throw himself over into the Abyss, the other side, the opposite of the Divine Name, where there was no divinity, no protection, only Qliphoth. From the Qliphoth, the devotee is to snatch a spark of holiness held there in exile. This may even be at the risk of offending the Qliphoth. Only the adept, the Zaddik, can accomplish this feat; only he can send his soul over into the other side, amid the other fallen souls.

Thus, talk of the ancient mystics invoking evil spirits and using Dark Forces may be merely bad translation or, even worse, bad understanding on the part of countless writers who misunderstand the uses of magic or the extremes of devotion. Picture, instead, your devoted Zaddik, risking his soul each morning in a ritual devotion. Picture the detachment, energy, and understanding such a practice can bring.

Picture the risk.

Try to picture the benefits.

CHAPTER 10

THE PATHS

THE STUDY OF the Paths on the Tree of Life is, in reality, the study of the relationships between the Holy Sephiroth. This is a subject, which, if treated fully, would make a book at least the size of this one, and so we cannot go into the sort of detailed discussion that is required. However, much can be done with a few hints and devoted meditation.

Each Path is a connecting link between the two Sephiroth it joins, as a road is a connection between two cities, and its nature is colored by them. For example, let us say that one road, and only one road, were to connect Paris and Berlin. Would not the people traveling that road be a mixture of French and German?

It is interesting to speculate that the authors of the Tarot may well have been conversant with, if not adepts in, the Kabbalah, since there are twenty-two letters in the Hebrew alphabet, twenty-two Paths on the Otz Chiim, and twenty-two Court cards in the Tarot.

It will be seen from the diagram of the full Tree (figure 1) that the Paths are numbered from 11 to 32, the first ten numbers being those of the Sephiroth. We can gain some insight into the natures of the Paths if we will be guided by the Tarot symbols assigned to each. Some consideration will be given also to the characteristics of the pair of Sephiroth connected by each Path.

11. This Path connects Kether and Chokmah. It is the course along which the precipitation flows from the First Sephirah to the Second. It partakes of the two natures, the static potential of Kether and the dynamic outpouring of force that is Chokmah. Its Tarot card is that of the Magician, which represents the creation of new things. Certainly this is symbolic of the Path, for new things, in fact, a new universe, has been created.

12. Connecting Kether and Binah, this Path has within its course the twin natures provided by these Sephiroth, the Crown, the Point which is the starting place of all creation; and Khorsia, the Throne, as well as Marah, the Great Sea. This is all made clear by the symbolism of the Tarot trump, the High Priestess, who is represented as seated upon a throne placed between two columns (Compassion and Austerity) showing that she partakes of both natures. She also wears a crown and has the Moon (Yesod) at her feet. She is representative of all that is female, and her Path is that of what might be called Crowned Womanhood, the perfect wife and mother, the understanding female. This is the Path to Kether by way of understanding, and transcending, Maya as the Eleventh Path is that carrying the direct vision of God through to Unity with God.

13. This is the Path that lies between Kether and Tiphareth, between the Absolute and the Avatar; the descent of God toward the material world. The respective Symbols are the Crown and the Cross, and the Titles are the Arik Anpin, or Vast Countenance, and the Zoar Anpin, or Lesser Countenance. It is the Path of the Mystic who has attained to the vision of the Chosen Ideal, or that aspect of God that he has taken as the object of his worship, and is now about to ascend to the topmost heights. There are three Paths up the center Column between Malkuth and Kether, and this is the last, and most difficult of the three. The Tarot trump symbolic of this Path is the Empress, and it might be well to remember here that there is nothing which says that the Son of God has to be masculine. Levels of consciousness, which is what the Sephiroth represent,

are not exclusively of either gender, but may be at one time considered as male and another as female, depending upon the circumstances of the particular force under observation and contemplation. The Empress signifies action combined with equilibrium.

14. We are now treading the Path between Chokmah and Binah, and also the course of the precipitation from the Second to the Third Sephirah. It links Wisdom and Understanding, thus making this the Path of Knowledge, the offspring of these two. It also conjoins the Celestial Father to the Celestial Mother, the Divine Lingam to the Divine Yoni, the Creative to the Receptive, force to form. Chokmah generates creation, and Binah produces it. But it is also to be remembered that Binah is not a merely passive receptacle, but stimulates the creativity of Chokmah. On the human level, the father impregnates the mother after she has stimulated him by her mere presence. The Fourteenth Path is the route by which both stimulation and creativity travel between Chokmah and Binah. The Tarot trump corresponding to this Path is the Emperor, also crowned as a sign of his residence within the Celestial Triangle. He holds a scepter and a globe, symbolizing the lingam and Heaven. The lingam is not only a sign for the phallus, but for an integration of both male and female, so that the Emperor is displaying the symbols of Celestial procreativity, or the function of the combined energies of Chokmah and Binah.

15. This is the Path uniting Chokmah with Tiphareth, the Celestial Father with the Son of God, Wisdom with Beauty. It is exemplified by the words of Christ: "I and my Father are one." While the Redeemer is the manifestation of the Absolute, he is generated by the Celestial Father. The Path also connects the Columns of Compassion and Serenity, two of the chief characteristics of the Avatar. Its Tarot trump is the High Priest, shown seated upon a throne, again between two columns. On his hands he wears white gloves, signifying their purity. He holds a scepter topped by a triple cross, whose six rounded ends, plus that of the tip, signify the

septenary groupings, such as the seven days of creation, and many others. Here, the reference is to the Seven Deadly Sins, and the Planetary Spheres by which to combat them: Pride, Shemesh (the Sun); Wrath, Madim (Mars); Envy, Kokab (Mercury); Lust, Nogah (Venus); Gluttony, Tzedek (Jupiter); Avarice, Shabbathai (Saturn); and Sloth, Levanah (the Moon). At the feet of the High Priest are two kneeling disciples, one dressed in red (activity) and the other in black (passivity). This is symbolic of the relationship between the Father and the Son: the passivity of the Son as he submits to his Father's activity. "The Father that dwelleth in me, he doeth the works."

16. The Sixteenth Path joins Chokmah and Chesed, Wisdom and Mercy, Power and Love. Both of these Sephiroth are located on the Column of Compassion, as is this Path, so we must expect that its message will be that of love and compassion. This is born out by its corresponding Tarot trump, the Lover, depicting a male figure, usually a representation of Hercules, and a female figure, sometimes—and more accurately—two female figures, since this refers to the legend which tells of how the Gods offered Hercules his choice of two women, Arete, personifying Virtue, and Kakia, Vice. At first, Hercules hesitates, but in the end, he choses Arete, who guides him through many pitfalls into the ways of rectitude. He is clad in parti-colored clothes, one side red, for activity, and the other green, for neutrality and indecision. When synthesized, the Lover represents integrity and love.

17. This is the Path connecting Tiphareth and Binah, Beauty and Understanding, The Celestial Mother and the Son. It also joins the Columns of Austerity and Serenity, or Discipline and Equilibrium. The Redeemer is usually regarded in his role of giving love and kindness, but he also brings discipline, for the follower of his way must indeed practice spiritual disciplines if he is to advance. The Tarot trump of the Seventeenth Path is the Chariot in which a Prince is riding. He wears a breastplate and holds a scepter. The Chariot is drawn by

what at first appears to be a pair of sphinxes, but which, upon further examination, is seen to be an amphisbaena, a fabulous poisonous serpent having a head at either end so that it tries to go in both directions, forward and back. The symbol here is of forces which must be brought into line—disciplined—in order to go forward. The breastplate signifies defence against base forces, the Avatar in his role of the Savior. It contains five golden studs, the Four Elements and the Ether. The Chariot is mounted on red wheels, in reference to the wheels in Ezekiel's vision. The Charioteer embodies the highest principles of man's nature, the goal which has been set for mankind by the Avatars.

18. Connecting Binah and Geburah, Understanding and Severity, this Path lies between the Sephiroth of the Celestial Mother and the Awe-inspiring Mother on the Column of Austerity. We will recall that one of the Titles assigned to Geburah is Din, Justice, and so it is quite fitting that the Tarot trump of the Eighteenth Path is Justice. The picture is of Justice personified, a young woman seated on a throne, holding in one hand a pair of scales, a symbol of equilibrium between good and evil, and in the other a sword, signifying the Word of God: "I came not to send peace, but a sword." Christ does not mean by this that he has come to bring war; he is saying that his mission is not one of making everyone feel comfortable, but of teaching them the Word of God, whether or not it disturbs them. This Justice is not the law of nations, the judicial weighing of guilt or innocence that we have come to associate with the familiar statue standing outside the courthouse. It is rather the inner judgment of oneself. As Thomas Hobbes said, in 1651: "A man's conscience and his judgment is the same thing." We have seen that Mother, in both aspects of Binah and Geburah, gives birth and, therefore, death. Here, now, is the added factor of self-judgment, which is the same as Karma. As the Hindus say, "Truly is Mahamaya wonderful. She spins this universe out of herself, as the spider spins her web, and like the spider, she withdraws the universe back into

herself. All the while, she holds the law of Karma in her hand."

19. This is the first Path traversing an area wholly below the Abyss; that is, having no connection with a Sephirah in the Celestial Triangle. It lies between Chesed and Geburah, Mercy and Severity; between Gedulah, Love, and Pachad, Fear. Again, it is the image of the corresponding Tarot trump that gives us the greatest insight into the message of this Path. It is the Hermit, an old man carrying a lantern in his right hand, reminiscen of Diogenes, who lived in a tub and carried a lantern about, saying he was searching for an honest man. His abode and his search signify humility and patience which result when one has both fear of God and Love for God. Having descended from the Celestial into the Moral Triangle, we find here the very height of morality as displayed by these virtues. The Hermit's cloak is dark on the outside, signifying the austerity of Geburah, but its inside is blue, representing the sky, the heavenly kingdom of Chesed, one of whose colors is blue.

20. The Twentieth Path is that which lies between Chesed and Tiphareth, Mercy and Beauty. We have here the relationship between Chesed, representing the Trinity of Brahma-Vishnu-Siva, and Tiphareth, the Avatar of Vishnu in any or all of his incarnations. One of the Images of Tiphareth is the Sacrificed God, and it is this aspect of the Sixth Sephirah that is featured here. Vishnu has come to Earth in the form of a man, once again to enact his role as the Redeemer. In the *Bhagavad Gita,* Krishna, the Avatar who teaches the sacred truths to Arjuna, the warrior prince, says:

> When virtue wanes and evil swells,
> I generate My human form.
> In every age I come again
> To free the righteous, quell all sin,
>
> And to proclaim the holy law.
> Who fathoms this My hallowed birth
> And selfless actions, comes to Me
> And after death is not reborn.

Further understanding comes with study of the Tarot trump, the Wheel of Fortune. It is an allegory based upon the symbolism of the wheel, which, in order to function properly, must be in balance, the equilibrium of the Column of Serenity. The Wheel is really the Wheel of Life, the Wheel of birth, death and rebirth; the Wheel to rescue mankind from which, the Avatar comes in human form in every age. The Wheel also represents the cyclical nature of man's life, his loves, hates, joys, sorrows, fortune and misfortune, or as Shakespeare put it: "The slings and arrows of outrageous fortune."

21. This is the Path lying between Chesed and Netzach, Mercy and Victory, and these are the qualities set forth in the corresponding Tarot trump, called Strength. The image is of a queen, crowned with a garland of flowers, clasping a lion that she has stunned to her breast, and holding his jaws open. The victory is, of course, that of the queen over the lion; the mercy is that she has not killed it, but is comforting it. This symbolizes the ancient belief of the alchemists that one must not—indeed one cannot—destroy what is inferior, but must transmute it into that which is superior. And this is the true Strength, the message of the Twenty-first Path, that if necessary, one must defeat the forces of destruction, but having done so, he must then strive to turn them into constructive forces. Much of man's climb toward civilization has been the story of this sort of transmutation, as for instance, his use of fire, a most destructive force, which, while still destructive, is used for constructive purposes. Another is the tremendous energy contained within the atom, which was first shown to the world as a frightfully destructive force, but which will be and, in fact, is being, used for constructive purposes. May Tzadkiel, the merciful Archangel of Chesed, grant that the day will come when the atom will be used only in a constructive manner.

22. Geburah and Tiphareth, Strength and Beauty, are the Holy Sephiroth connected by the Twenty-second Path. We read in the text of the *Sepher Yetzirah* for Geburah: ". . . allying itself to Binah," and this indicates

a lower representation of the Mother of the Universe, the Mother of the Redeemer, Tiphareth. This is the Sphere of Mary, mother of Christ, of Maya, mother of the Buddha, and of Devaki, mother of Krishna. The precipitation runs from Chesed through Geburah to Tiphareth, or from Vishnu through Lakshmi (and the Goddess' human form, Mary, Maya, Devaki) to the Avatar. The Tarot trump for the Twenty-second Path does not seem at first sight to be at all appropriate, for it is the Hanged Man, the most enigmatic of them all. However, let us see if there is something about the Hanged Man that might fit our purpose. The image is that of a young man suspended by one ankle from a scaffold, sometimes in the form of a crossbar supported by two trees, symbolizing the Columns of Compassion and Austerity, with the youth as the third Column of Serenity, the seat of Tiphareth. Hanging as he does, he signifies a Deity suspended between Heaven and Earth, free of all mundane influences. Being upside down, he symbolizes purification, since his position reverses the natural order of things. The image is akin to the myth of Odin, the Norse God, who hanged himself as a sacrifice. In the *Havamal* we read:

> This do I know:
> I have been hanging
> From this storm-whipped tree
> For nine nights unceasing,
> Wounded by the spear,
> A sacrifice to Odin:
> Myself offered to myself.

The interpretation of this trump is that the man does not live the ordinary life of this Earth, but a life of mysticism and a higher reality. His arms are tied together, and in his hands he holds opened sacks out of which gold coins fall to the ground, the meaning being, of course, that he has rare treasures for those who come to him. This Path is thus a two-way street; the Avatar is descended from his Mother, but we who are to climb the heights must pass through the Son to his Mother, from Tiphareth to Geburah.

23. This Path is the way between Geburah and Hod, Strength and Glory. Here is the Mother and her first offspring, the Hermaphrodite, who later is divided into man and woman. The Tarot trump corresponding to the Twenty-third Path is also most enigmatic on first consideration, being that of Death. The image is that of a Skeleton, but wielding his scythe toward the left, contrary to the normal manner. There is another departure from the norm: his bones are not the natural grey tone one would expect, but pink. Around him the ground is covered with the remains of those he has scythed down, but here, again, these parts do not have the appearance of the dead, for the faces seem alive and the hands are able to perform their normal functions. We have then, an image of conflicting symbols, death and not-death, or life in death. Heretofore, we have considered life as the beginning of death, as was discussed in the section dealing with Geburah. Now we have an opposite doctrine, that death is the beginning of life, or perhaps it would be better to say that death is the source of life. Death is but one of the way-stations on the road of birth, death and rebirth, the interminable round from which we can only escape by the doorway of Kether, the ultimate exit from the Tree of Life, as it was the primal entrance into the Tree. Geburah, whose other name is Severity, and Hod, whose name is Glory, are joined by this Path, whose better name is Transformation.

24. The Twenty-fourth Path joins Tiphareth and Netzach, Beauty and Victory. We have previously seen that the Planetary Sphere of Netzach is Venus, and this Goddess, in her higher form, represents pure love, which is most appropriate in her relations with the Avatar. Innocence, the innocence of the pure in heart, is further typified by the Magical Images of the Child and the Naked Woman. This is exemplified by the story of Sukadeva, the young saint, who had received the highest illumination and was always conscious of being one with

God. Bent on renouncing the world, he left his home, and his father Vyasa, also a great sage, ran after him to bring him back. Just as he caught sight of his son, the boy passed a pool where a number of young women were bathing quite naked. As Sukadeva went by, the young women made no effort to cover themselves, any more than if he had been another woman. But when Vyasa came into view, they quickly scrambled to dress themselves. He said to them: "Here I am, an old man, and yet you are shy before me, but you were not so with my handsome son. Why is that?" And one of them replied for the rest: "You are old, it is true, but you still have some worldly thoughts, and so we felt some embarrassment. However, Sukadeva has only one thought, that he is one with God. In him is no thought of male and female, and so we were not shy." The corresponding Tarot trump is Temperance. It contains the image of a winged angel, a star on her forehead, pouring water from a silver pitcher into a golden one, which is symbolic of transformation from the sphere of the Moon to that of the Sun, or from the level of transitory forms to that of stable and fixed form, in other words, from the astral to that of Earth. This is the best possible description of the nature of the Twenty-fourth Path.

25. This is the Path leading from Tiphareth to Yesod, from Beauty to the Foundation, from the etheric to the mundane. It lies entirely within the central Column of Serenity, and this bespeaks a state of equilibrium. We may, therefore, be permitted some questioning of the suitability of the corresponding Tarot trump, the Devil, which, according to Oswald Wirth, in his book, *Le Tarot des Imagiers du Moyen Age,* is related to the instincts and to desire in all its passionate forms, the magic arts, disorder and perversion. We are not to be permitted any prettification of the image; it must be dealt with as it is. And the image is not a pretty one, being that of the idol of the Knights Templars, Baphomet, whose name was composed of three abbreviations, in reverse: Tem. ohp. Ab, using the letters here capitalized, TEMpli Omnium Hominum Pacis ABhas, "the father of the temple of

universal peace among men." He has a torch between his horns, which again brings us to the symbolism of the Three Columns, the torch, of course, a sign of equilibrium. It has human hands and female breasts, signifying work and reproduction, "In the sweat of thy face shalt thou eat bread . . . in sorrow thou shalt bring forth children," the curse, but also the way of redemption, pronounced by God in the Garden of Eden. It is to be remembered that Lucifer was also a Son of God (Tiphareth) who fell from grace into the physical world (Yesod), and his fall was by way of the Twenty-fifth Path. If Lucifer's sin was that of pride, the way back to Tiphareth must be that of humility.

26. Connecting Tiphareth and Hod, Beauty and Glory, the Son of God and the first son of man, the hermaphrodite—mystically speaking. In *The Secret Doctrine*, Madam Blavatsky says that the first race in physical form, the Third Root Race, is hermaphroditic, producing offspring out of itself, its lowest descent into life being that of the Astral Plane, and Hod is on that plane. The Tarot trump of this Path is the Tower Struck by Lightning, a most adverse card in divination, but with much to tell us as a symbol of this Path. The Tower is to be identified with the Column of Austerity, the seat of birth and death. It is to be taken as an image of a human being, since its bricks are flesh-colored. The lightning, having struck the top of the Tower, equivalent to the head, and the two figures who either are pictured as falling from it, or being struck by pieces of falling masonry, are a king and the architect of the Tower. This brings us to the allegory of the Tower of Babel, wherein the sin of pride brings about disaster. When faced with the heady wine of combined Beauty and Glory, one will be only human if he succumbs to the twin images, falling into the sin of pride. Again, however, we hear the message of humility; it is the only way of negotiating the Path between Tiphareth and Hod.

27. This is the first Path to lie wholly below the Veil of the Temple, being the base, although on top, of the Mundane Triangle, and the course of the precipitation

from Netzach to Hod, Victory and Glory, Venus and Mercury, the Earth Mother and her child, the hermaphrodite. The Tarot trump assigned to this Path is the Stars, and it carries a symbolism directly related to that Path. Depicted is a naked woman (the Magical Image of Netzach is a beautiful naked woman), kneeling beside a pool (symbolic of a Sephirah, as we have seen) and pouring water (precipitation) into the pool, from a golden jar held in her right hand. In her left hand is another jar of silver, from which she pours the life-giving water upon the dry land, thus causing the arid soil to be fertile. Above her is a bright star (the Element of Fire) and several lesser ones shining in the heavens (the Element of Air) upon her actions, the Elements of Water and Earth being obvious.

28. The Twenty-eighth Path connects Netzach and Yesod, Victory and the Foundation, and the Magical Images of a beautiful naked woman and a beautiful naked man. The Planetary Spheres are those of Venus and the Moon, the significance of which we are about to discover, for the corresponding Tarot trump is the Moon. Depicted is the Moon in the form of a silvery disk having the outlines of a woman, which casts a dim light upon the Earth. Beneath it is a large red crab, its claws raised toward the Moon. There are also two watchdogs baying at the Moon, as if to protect the Sun. Behind them are two castles, or towers, again flesh-colored, the left and right hand Columns, the central Column being the Moon, itself. The concept is of visions, those seen dimly as by the lunar light, which, if false, that is, based on imagination alone and not having reality behind them, will be devoured by the crab, who is the symbol of the scavenger disposing of rejected matter, physical and spiritual. The concept symbolized here is of the dangers in transitory visions, unstable ideas as to what is Real, and the abandonment of reason. And yet, the dogs who are guarding the "Solar Way" of reason and objectivity, indicate that this is the Path of the "Lunar Way" of intuition and subjectivity, which will lead us from the Foundation to Victory.

29. This is the Path lying between Netzach and Malkuth, Victory and the Kingdom, Venus and the Sphere of the Elements. The Tarot trump associated with the Twenty-ninth Path is the Sun, and it will be recalled that the text in the *Sepher Yetzirah* tells us that: "It [Malkuth] illuminates the radiance of every light, and causes an influence to flow down from the Prince of Countenances, the Archangel of Kether." The image portrayed is variously one of a naked child riding a white horse, or a young couple in a green field. Whichever of these is shown, they are benefitting from the spiritual influence of the Sun, which, as the symbol of constancy, gives a clear view of reality, rather than the dim view of the imagination. The Sun is also the symbolic source of illumination in the spiritual nature, the purification of the senses so that they may perceive the Truth. Our Path, from the material Earth to the realm of spiritual love is lighted by the Sun of Kether.

30. The Thirtieth Path is that which connects Hod and Yesod. Glory and the Kingdom, the Magical Image of the Hermaphrodite, with that of the naked man. This symbolizes the advent of the Fourth Root Race, as described by Madame Blavatsky in *The Secret Doctrine,* from the unisexual being to the bisexual human. This Path is one of life and death, both physical and spiritual, as will be seen from its Tarot trump, the Day of Judgment. Depicted is the Angel of Judgment Day, Gabriel, who is also the Archangel of Yesod. Gabriel is sounding his trumpet, and the tombs of the dead open to permit those within to rise, hands clasped in prayer, for their appearance before the throne of God. But there is more to this image than that of the Last Day. Gabriel, the Archangel of the Moon, is pictured here with the symbol of the Sun on his brow, and this warns us that there is something more profound to be said. Death is not only that of the body, but in a mystic sense, means the death of the soul, and its tomb is the body sealed by its desires. When Gabriel blows his trumpet and sheds his light upon mankind, those who are inspired seek higher levels. The resurrection of the soul leads to illumination.

31. This Path lies between Hod and Malkuth, Glory and the Kingdom. These names are surely reminiscent of the final words of the Lord's Prayer, lacking only "Power," which is supplied by the Image of Yesod, the strong young man. Thus, the last three terms of the Prayer are the Three Last Sephiroth, Malkuth, Yesod and Hod. Malkuth is also the kingdom of the Fifth Root Race of Madame Blavatsky, the race that now is dominant on Earth, which we call the Human Race. The Tarot trump of the Thirty-first Path is the World, portrayed as a nude young woman, encircled by a garland of roses and lillies. At each corner of the card is a symbol of one of the Four Elements. The young woman is holding two small sticks which signify the polarity of all created things, force and form, energy and matter. The roses in the garland are symbolic of earthly love and the lillies of purity. This suggests that the Thirty-first Path is that of the struggle that lies before man if he is to raise himself from the purely mundane to a slightly higher level.

32. This is the last of the Paths on the Tree of Life, the way between Yesod and Malkuth, the Foundation and the Kingdom. In the section dealing with Yesod, it was said that it is the sphere of Maya, that erroneous cognition of the world by the human senses that "creates" what we think of as the "real world." Maya has been called "illusion," but Maya is more than that. There is a world, but our faulty sensing of it prevents us from seeing it as it is. Thus, Maya has been called the Mother of the Universe, for it is Maya that has "created" the world in which we think we live. That world is the sphere of Malkuth, which has received the precipitations of all the other Sephiroth through Yesod, and Yesod, according to the text in the *Sepher Yetzirah,* "verifies and rectifies the plan of their representations, and orders the unity in which they were planned."

The Thirty-second Path is to be considered as not only the way by which the physical universe is precipitated, but the beginning of the way of humanity on its climb back to the heights. The Kabbalists call the way that leads straight up the central Column, from Malkuth to Kether, the Path of the Arrow, and the first station on this Path is Yesod, the next being Tiphareth. If the aspirant should travel the road to Hod, he will, having accomplished it, attain to a mastery of the images of Yesod, for Hod is the sphere of magic, and one must attain to the next highest sphere before he can master that through which he has merely passed.

This is the course of the occultist, but the Path of the Arrow is that of the mystic, and the aspirant must choose between them according to his own nature and preference; those who wish to acquire the powers of magic will take the occult road, and those who care little for these powers, but want only to achieve illumination and liberation will follow the Path of the Arrow. For either the occultist or the mystic, the first step is the Thirty-second Path, known to some as the Cross of Suffering, because it is a difficult road, primarily for the reason that it is the first one. To raise one's consciousness from the material to the astral plane is far more difficult than it is to transcend the astral to those beyond, for we are surrounded by, and filled with, the signs and tokens of the material world and these have a very strong hold upon us indeed.

The corresponding Tarot trump is the Fool, whose meaning, as suggested by Eliphas Levi, is the microcosm, the sum of All-in-All. This would seem to be a rather apt description of the Thirty-second Path, which is the way from Yesod into Malkuth, and also the way from Malkuth back to Yesod. The Fool is dressed in the usual costume of the jester, multi-colored to suggest the Elements and the Four Worlds. He carries a staff over his shoulder, from which is suspended a sack, signifying the burden of mental concepts, most of which are at least partially false, with which man loads himself. The Hindus have a story that illustrates this idea. A man was walking along a road, carrying a heavy burden on his back. Another man asked him: "Where are you going?" "I don't know." "Where do you come from?" "I don't know." "What is in your bundle?" "I don't know." "If you don't know what you are carrying, or why you are carrying it, or where you are taking it, why don't you lay it down?" "I don't know." This is the Fool and his burden, but there is hope for him, that is, for mankind, because the image includes a small purple tulip, expressing the spiritual nature, and he is wearing a gold belt emblazoned with the twelve signs of the Zodiac. The Gypsies say that the Fool "possesses the foolishness of God, which is greater than the wisdom of men." In other words, the Fool is nobody's fool. He is a most fitting representation of man, for man is frequently, if not most often, a fool, his stupidities achieving a certain magnificence in their abundance, but he is also capable of achieving the heights of spirituality. For those who fear that mankind is on the verge of blowing itself and its world into fine particles of radioactive dust, the Fool reassures us that although man is foolish enough to try it, he will fail. The Tree of Life is not about to be chopped down; it cannot be destroyed by even the most foolish, for the Tree has brought forth its fruit, and the fruit is not greater than the Tree. The Garden of Eden is not a place; it does not exist in a certain location. Eden is a state of consciousness, and the Tree of Life stands well-guarded in Eden, protected from the assaults of even the most evil-intentioned.

CHAPTER 11

WORK UPON THE TREE

HOW DOES ONE meditate upon the Tree of Life?

We do not stop with the gaining of practical data, since this would be of little avail, no more than a student could call himself a qualified physician if he has merely read all the textbooks and successfully passed all his examinations.

Having gained the factual knowledge of the Sephiroth and the paths, one must set himself to meditating upon the Tree. He does not use his conscious mind, since he would then be bound to an intellectual viewing of the pictograph and might well find himself trying somehow to force some sort of intelligible response from it. But will he invite his subconscious mind to take over and permit a sort of free associational process to prevail. It is almost as though he were in a dream, the sort of dream in which the subconscious mind follows the illogical logic of the dream state, shifting from one eidolon to another, one abstraction to another, one concept to another. To achieve this may seem a quite arduous task at first, but then, no one has ever promised that the occult path would be easy. It is difficult to express the process in precise terms, perhaps even impossible to do so. But then, have you ever thought of how truly difficult it would be to describe—using words alone—the process of taking one simple step in walking? However, one may give hints of the method to serve as mental and spiritual guideposts pointing out the way. Here are a few of these roadside signs:

1. It is, of course, impossible to make the mind a blank; the harder one tries, the fuller the mind becomes. It is like the story of the pseudoholy man, who promised his disciples instant liberation if they would refrain from thinking about sex for as little as five minutes. The students, who, up to that moment, had not been thinking of sex at all, having been more interested in their spiritual advancement, at once began furiously trying not to think of sex, and the result, as we could have foretold, was that their minds were filled with thoughts of sex to the exclusion of everything else. Therefore, we do not make our minds blank; instead, we try merely to calm the waves of worldly thinking, and fix our vision upon the Tree.

2. The mind, of course, will wander; we are not yet adepts, and cannot expect to achieve instant concentration. When it wanders, we gently draw it back to a contemplation of the Tree. This is repeated over and over again, until the wandering is less and less frequent. A time will come when it will not wander at all. This is a promise.

3. One of the oldest of methods for taming the mind during its travels away from the desired object, is to say to it (as though it were something apart from yourself): "Very well, then, go ahead and wander, and I will just sit quietly here and watch you." The remark enclosed in parentheses is quite true; the mind is not the self, but one of the organs of the self. One can stand apart from the conscious mind. If he could not, he would not have the awareness of his own thoughts. There must be something other than the mind to be aware of what the mind is up to, and that is the self. As we watch our minds roaming over hill and dale (making no attempt to prevent these travels), a strange phenomenon occurs. The mind, as though inhibited by being observed, comes back from its hills and dales and submits to its master's orders. Then it may be fixed, if only for a time, upon the object of meditation.

4. We have now arrived at the point where we may devote at least part of the meditation period to a contemplation of the Tree. This meditation is not to be discursive; that is, it is not to be of the sort that would be concerned with reason and factual knowledge. True, we have gained some knowledge of the Sephiroth, the forces which preside over them and reside in them, and their relationship to each other, and this is to serve as a foundation for meditation, but this is not the object, or the subject, of that meditation. The object is the Tree itself; there is no subject. One observes the Tree; that is all. It is almost inevitable that the mind will begin a pattern of patternless free association, and out of this will emerge, in time, an intuitive knowledge of the Tree and all—or at least much—of what it has to tell us. When we have learned all it has to tell us, we will have been transported to the Thousand Petaled Lotus of the Sahasrara Chakra, which is Kether, the goal of all our struggles, total illumination.

5. What follows is a statement that can only be fully comprehended by an adept. However, it is a clue for even the beginner. As he contemplates the Tree of Life, he should look into the pictograph, seeing not merely the surface of the drawing, but diving beneath the surface. As the days pass, he will dive ever deeper, until he finally becomes immersed in it. Then, and only then, will the Tree begin to yield up its secrets to him. Is this not a strange way to be speaking of a simple, flat, two dimensional drawing? Not at all. If that is all the Tree means, then it obviously has nothing to tell. But, suppose we were to take this attitude about poetry, or music. A poem is constructed of words; a symphony of sounds, noises if you will. There is nothing intrinsically beautiful or magical in plain words or unrelated sounds. But put those words together as the great poets have, and read them as they were meant to be read, with a sympathetic understanding of the pictures and emotions they were designed to invoke, and you may well be overcome by the beauty and, yes, the magic, those conglomerations of letters can conjure up. Or take any

single note of music set down on paper, a funny-looking small black oval, with a tail attached, standing on, above or below a set of lines that look as though they had been drawn by a five-tyned fork, and it will have very little to say to us. Even when it is sounded by a musical instrument, it does not make much of an impression, but let a great orchestra play a large group of such funny-looking marks, as set down by a master composer, and there are moments when the very gates of Heaven seem about to open. Poems composed of letters strung into words, and symphonies composed of notes strung into harmonies, melodies and rhythmic patterns, are pictographs in exactly the same way that the Otz Chiim is a pictograph, although the Tree has infinitely more to say to us than do poems and symphonies. So, dive deep into the Tree. It is all there.

6. Even more important than a study of the whole Tree will be the study of the individual Sephiroth. When one is about to embark on this, and before he begins his meditation upon it, he should first invoke the presence of that áspect of God which has precipitated the Sephirah under observation, calling upon Him by the Divine Name appropriate to the Sephirah. Our purpose in doing this is not only to seek his assistance, but also to prevent the negative influences of the Qliphoth from interfering. To invoke the aid of the Deity, one should call silently upon Him by the Divine Name and attempt to put himself into psychic and spiritual communion with Him. Having done this, one is next to invoke the Archangel of the Sephirah, praying him to enjoin the Angelic Host of that sphere to assist in the study. This will prove to be of immeasurable help in attaining the necessary understanding.

7. It must be repeated, over and over again, that there is only one God, and that the Archangels, Angels, and all the Heavenly Hosts are not individual beings, but a convenient way of communicating with the various powers and influences of the universe. If one fully comprehends this, he may proceed to act as though there actually were such Beings. It is far simpler to

invoke such a Being than it is to try to recall all of the contents, so to speak, of the package of attributes which that Being represents, particularly when one has stored in his memory all the assigned powers and influences of that Being, just as it may sometimes be easier to think of Santa Claus than to recall all those characteristics the Spirit of Christmas represents.

8. Of course, any study of an individual Sephirah yields very little unless one contemplates it in relation to the other Sephiroth with which it is associated. Netzach can only be grasped in its affiliation to Hod, and Yesod to both of these, for example. We have seen that this relationship is best expressed by the Paths that connect them, and it is the Paths which must be understood, as well as the Sephiroth themselves, if we are to make any progress on the Tree. There may come an objection at this point to the effect that there is just too much material for the memory to hold, but this can only be said by one who is not aware of the almost infinite capacity of the mind. This might be true, if, after one or two readings of the material presented in this book, one were asked to take an examination in it. But we are, as has been pointed out, to follow a course of unconscious free association, and when we contemplate a Sephirah or a Path in this manner, all those things we have come to learn about it will step forward as they are required. There must be no straining to remember, or we will bounce back into a state of conscious awareness. There must be a resistance to any use of the mental faculties in the way they would be employed in trying to reason something out. Let us say it again and again: we merely contemplate the Tree. It will tell us what we need to know.

9. After one has contemplated the Tree faithfully for some time, he will begin to take comfort from the mere fact of its simple presence, even if he is not meditating upon it at that moment. By his work on it, he has given it a place in his life, he has, in fact, made it a part of his life. It gets up with him in the morning and goes to bed with him at night. He is never alone, for it is always with

him, and at this point, he can call himself a true student of the Otz Chiim.

10. One should start his work by contemplating Malkuth and the Thirty-second Path, leading to Yesod. Nothing is to be gained by starting somewhere else on the Tree, for no other Sephirah will yield up its wisdom until the aspirant has prepared himself for its study. We might use the simile of a scholastic education: one is not ready for the second grade until he has accomplished the work of the first, and so on. The child is ready to progress to the next grade when he has taken and passed the appropriate examinations. For the aspirant on the Tree, one will know he is ready to advance when he has been given the vision associated with the Sephirah he has been contemplating. However, he is not the master of that Sephirah, or level of consciousness, but has become the master of the Sephirah next below. One masters each Sephirah as he attains to the vision of the next higher level.

11. If the aspirant wishes to perform the operation known as "Rising on the Planes," which has also been called the Path of the Arrow, he must raise his consciousness from Malkuth to Yesod, thence to Tiphareth and, finally, to Kether. This is not to be undertaken by one who has not mastered the various Sephiroth and Paths on the Tree, not because it is forbidden, but impossible of execution at the outset. The least requirement for this operation is that all the Sephiroth, up to and including Tiphareth, must have been entered. One may then either pursue his way from Tiphareth to Geburah, to Chesed, from Geburah to Chesed, to Binah, to Chokmah, from Binah to Chokmah, and finally to Kether, or he may try the last part of the Path of the Arrow, going directly from Tiphareth to Kether. There is another reason why one must be prepared for this journey. When he realizes what arrival in Kether implies: "And Enoch walked with God: and he was not; for God Took him," the aspirant might pull back at the last moment, bringing all his efforts to naught. One must be an adept indeed to accept the idea that he will reach the

heights, and having done so, will cease to exist. Of course, no one is in any danger of this if he is not prepared to accept it, for his having the least concern about his own existence will prevent him from crossing the great abyss and entering into the Void. He may rise to Kether by the way of a steady climb up the Tree, and his experience then will be of just touching the outer fringes of the First Sephirah, in which he may see a blinding white light and, perhaps, lose all capacity for conscious though for a short while. This is the highest state of illumination to be reached by man without his going out of earthly existence.

This, then, is the Sacred Kabbalah, whose beginnings are shrouded by the mists of time and whose ending will come only with the ending of humanity. But I am in error; this is not *the* Sacred Kabbalah, in the sense that this book does not contain the whole of it. On the contrary, there is much more than can be bound within the covers of any book, no matter how large. What remains untold is what the aspirant himself will add, the pages he will write out of his experiences upon the Tree. If these pages are not written, then the book is just a book, having no more significance than the printed recipes in an unused cookbook.

So there is work to be done. The gifts of the Tree are not to be bestowed for the mere asking. One must struggle to attain them, as he would struggle if he heard that a vast treasure was to be found in a place to which access was most difficult. Well, here are gold and jewels in abundance, and the sacrifices that one must make to obtain them are small when compared to those who go in search of material wealth. As it is written in the *Bhagavad Gita:*

> To meditate is sacrifice
> Beyond all sacrificial rites.
> The realm of action leads to truth,
> To wisdom and enlightenment.

"For the Millions" Series

The
"For the Millions"
Series

ALCHEMY by William Leo—A modern look at what was probably the first hard science the world has ever known, beginning as a cross between chemistry and philosophy, with a goal of changing base metals into gold, developing universal cures for disease, and establishing ways to prolong human life indefinitely.

AMERICAN INDIAN RELIGIONS by John Major Hurdy—An informative, accurate focus on the use of mysticism, the development of supernatural talents, and the means by which peoples of influential tribes integrate their religion into everyday living.

AN ASTROLOGY PRIMER by Carl Payne Tobey—One of America's great experts on astrology presents a fascinating introduction to the subject. "A rich collection of knowledge." Phoenix, Arizona *Gazette*.

BORDERLINE ODDITIES edited by Shelly Lowenkopf—An anthology of accounts of people with strange abilities, beliefs, and ways of communications. A good high school, junior college, adult education supplement to spur reading interest.

CHARMS, SPELLS, AND CURSES by Victor Banis—A treasure trove of witchery, villainy, and black and white magic. Ancient names for roots and other ingredients are modernized.

COMPLETE HAND READING by Edith Niles—An illustrated, up-to-date study showing how to use the entire human hand in personality and character readings.

COMPLETE I CHING by Edward Albertson—Has all the necessary data to launch a basic understanding of the world's most famous oracle. Featured in *TV Guide*.

DEVELOPING ESP by Patrick Somerset—A successful introduction to the techniques for developing and testing various ESP abilities.

DOWSING, DIVINING RODS, AND WATER WITCHES by Howard V. Chambers—The first important book in ten years to show how dowsing works, how it began, who has the ability to dowse, and what tools they use.

ESP by Susy Smith—America's favorite psychic researcher opens the door to the world of ESP abilities and phenomena. "Should intrigue skeptic and believer." San Diego, CA *Union*.

FAMOUS GHOSTS, PHANTOMS, AND POLTERGEISTS by Andrew Tackaberry—Exciting accounts of beings from other worlds who return to earth to seek revenge and . . . occasionally just fun. "An excellent primer." *The Spirit Quaterly*.

HANDWRITING ANALYSIS by Dorothy Sara—A noted specialist gives tips on how to judge character, psyche from handwriting. Profusely illustrated.

HAUNTED HOUSES by Susy Smith—A guided tour through modern haunted houses. "Scary but good." Bill Wolff, CBS radio.

HYPNOTISM by Clayton Matthews—How hypnotism works, how it can be used in connection with strengthening ESP abilities.

LOST CONTINENTS by Marilyn S. Pierce—Amazing stories, valid theories, and shrewd, cautious appraisals of the former continents of Mu, Lemuria, and Atlantis. Complete with maps and new findings.

MENTAL TELEPATHY AND ESP POWERS by Max Holbourne—A definitive introduction to the kinds of telepathic powers now on record. "Quite valuable for the lay person." Christian Research Institute.

MIRACLE CURES by G. Victor Levesque—Stories of modern day individuals who experienced cures of illness after medical authorities gave up hope on them.

MORE ESP by Susy Smith—New stories of ESP sent Miss Smith by readers of her first book.

MORE TAROT SECRETS by Joanne Sydney Bennet—Additional methods for quick readings with the 78-card tarot deck, prepared by the author of the introductory tarot book in this series.

MYSTICISM by Norman Winski—A popular, easy-to-digest book showing how today's living is enhanced through use of mystical thought and mystical techniques of communication.

AN OCCULT DICTIONARY compiled by Howard V. Chambers—Hundreds of terms, names, definitions. "A big seller . . . a basic guide to the occult." *McCall's*

OUT-OF-BODY EXPERIENCES by Susy Smith—Actual stories of individuals who can detach from their bodies and move about at will.

PHRENOLOGY by Howard V. Chambers—The first modern work in years on the famous "science" of head reading. Entertaining, informative, amazingly useful and provocative.

PROPHECY by Edward Albertson—Actual accounts of past and present individuals who can forecast the events of the future.

PSYCHIC SELF-IMPROVEMENT by William Wolff—The famous Concept Therapy story that shows how to heal with ideas.

PSYCHIC TALENTS by Clayton Matthews—Eye-opening accounts of people who have found strange, effective ways to make ESP work special wonders for them.

REINCARNATION by Susy Smith—America's most popular psychical researcher takes on the most controversial occult subject of all and draws some conclusions, offers some information you won't want to miss.

SCIENCE OF MIND by Doris Heather Buckley—A dynamic approach to living and believing in the world of today. Makes the mind draw in power like a strong radio, tuned in on The Source.

SCIENTOLOGY by Walter Braddeson—A step-by-step introduction to the new and personal emotional discipline that may help you join those who have expanded their abilities.

SEANCES AND SENSITIVES by Edward Albertson—Accounts of world-famous mediums past and present; case histories involving some of the greatest trance mediums of all time.

SECRET PSYCHIC ORGANIZATIONS by Clayton Matthews—Inside secrets that have been kept for years, sometimes even centuries, by psychic organizations and religions throughout the world.

SECRETS OF EGYPT by Marilyn S. Pierce—Delves into Egyptian mysteries of the past and shows how to develop the same mysterious abilities as Egyptian royalty. Also shows you how to write your name, other items, in hieroglyphics.

SPIRIT COMMUNICATION by Doris Heather Buckley—Accounts of dealings with recently dead beings and their adjustments to the spirit world.

SPIRITUAL YOGA by Edward Albertson—A complete introduction to spiritual and contemplative yoga, showing how each path can be used for results.

A SUPERNATURAL PRIMER by Susy Smith—An exciting, case history-illustrated introduction to the world of spirits, strange beings, and mysterious activities.

TAROT by Joanne Sydney Bennett—An introduction to the 78-card fortune telling deck that is one of the most ancient and accurate sources of divination known to man. Complete instructions. Also shows how to case readings from regular bridge deck.

UFO's by Howard V. Chambers—The ideal introduction to the lore of unidentified flying objects. Hundreds of case histories, details of sightings, etc. "A familiarization manual for new fans," Hartford, Conn. *Courant.*

UNDERSTANDING DREAMS by James Bellaugh—Hundreds of listings and modern dream subjects, all with clear, up-to-date interpretations. Especially good in symbolism, fantasy, and ESP tendencies.

UNDERSTANDING JUNG by Norman Winski—A simplified introduction to the main writings and occult ideas of the most original and penetrating psychiatric thinker of modern years. Nothing like this guide available anywhere at any cost.

UNDERSTANDING THE SUFIS by Howard V. Chambers—A simplified introduction to the "Whirling Dirvishes," Moslem mysticism, mideastern alchemy, and magic.

UNDERSTANDING ZEN by Edward Albertson—A unique, all-new text that shows how this, the most popular of Eastern religions, can be learned and used effectively by persons of all ages.

UNITY by Kam Lytton—An introduction to one of the most powerful and popular modern religions. Shows how to attract success, health, self-confidence. A SELECTION OF THE UNITY BOOK CLUB.

VEDANTA by Edward Albertson—Written by an actual follower of this modern offshoot of the Hindu faith, this introduction is geared to the Western reader who wishes to follow in the footsteps of the great gurus and learn the revelations that attracted such famous 20th century minds as Huxley, Isherwood, Heard, etc.

VOODOO by Jacques D'Argent—Based on information given the author by actual informants who practice and believe in the effectiveness of this eclectic religion. Details of voodoo personages, charms, spells, cures, etc.

WEREWOLVES, SHAPESHIFTERS, AND SKINWALKERS by John Major Hurdy—A modern introduction to people who can assume the shape and characters of animals, what they want, how they "work."

WITCHCRAFT by Marika Kriss—One of the most unique approaches to witchcraft in print, this introduction takes an anthropological and functional look at one of the most misunderstood subjects in history and makes some of the most sensible conclusions in print.